Digital Music P

Gergely Szigeti

Digital Music Processing Experiments

Building a Musical Information System: Tool Development in MATLAB

VDM Verlag Dr. Müller

Impressum/Imprint (nur für Deutschland/ only for Germany)

Bibliografische Information der Deutschen Nationalbibliothek: Die Deutsche Nationalbibliothek verzeichnet diese Publikation in der Deutschen Nationalbibliografie; detaillierte bibliografische Daten sind im Internet über http://dnb.d-nb.de abrufbar.

Alle in diesem Buch genannten Marken und Produktnamen unterliegen warenzeichen-, marken- oder patentrechtlichem Schutz bzw. sind Warenzeichen oder eingetragene Warenzeichen der jeweiligen Inhaber. Die Wiedergabe von Marken, Produktnamen, Gebrauchsnamen, Handelsnamen, Warenbezeichnungen u.s.w. in diesem Werk berechtigt auch ohne besondere Kennzeichnung nicht zu der Annahme, dass solche Namen im Sinne der Warenzeichen- und Markenschutzgesetzgebung als frei zu betrachten wären und daher von jedermann benutzt werden dürften.

Coverbild: www.purestockx.com

Verlag: VDM Verlag Dr. Müller Aktiengesellschaft & Co. KG
Dudweiler Landstr. 99, 66123 Saarbrücken, Deutschland
Telefon +49 681 9100-698, Telefax +49 681 9100-988, Email: info@vdm-verlag.de

Herstellung in Deutschland:
Schaltungsdienst Lange o.H.G., Berlin
Books on Demand GmbH, Norderstedt
Reha GmbH, Saarbrücken
Amazon Distribution GmbH, Leipzig
ISBN: 978-3-639-18163-0

Imprint (only for USA, GB)

Bibliographic information published by the Deutsche Nationalbibliothek: The Deutsche Nationalbibliothek lists this publication in the Deutsche Nationalbibliografie; detailed bibliographic data are available in the Internet at http://dnb.d-nb.de .

Any brand names and product names mentioned in this book are subject to trademark, brand or patent protection and are trademarks or registered trademarks of their respective holders. The use of brand names, product names, common names, trade names, product descriptions etc. even without a particular marking in this works is in no way to be construed to mean that such names may be regarded as unrestricted in respect of trademark and brand protection legislation and could thus be used by anyone.

Cover image: www.purestockx.com

Publisher:
VDM Verlag Dr. Müller Aktiengesellschaft & Co. KG
Dudweiler Landstr. 99, 66123 Saarbrücken, Germany
Phone +49 681 9100-698, Fax +49 681 9100-988, Email: info@vdm-publishing.com

Printed in the U.S.A.
Printed in the U.K. by (see last page)
ISBN: 978-3-639-18163-0

University of Veszprém

Department of Process Engineering
and
Department of Information Technology
Faculty of Information Technology

Diploma Thesis

Building a Musical Information System: Tool Development in MATLAB

Gergely Szigeti

Supervisors:

dr. János Abonyi
dr. Ferenc Péter Pach

Tutor:

Emil Mógor

2005

ACKNOWLEDGMENTS

I would like to thank my supervisor dr. János Abonyi for help and his endless patience.

I would like to thank my friend and supervisor dr. Ferenc Péter Pach to spur me and for help in $\LaTeX$.

Thanks to Emil Mógor for his indispensable advices.

Thanks to Suresh Joel for the test tones and test program.

Many thanks to all the composers and performers for the songs I have worked with.

And last but not least many thanks to the Free Software Foundation, the Debian Community and the thousands of volunteers to develop Debian GNU/Linux and great free softwares.

Contents

Contents

Preface

Musical transcription is a widespread research area of data processing since 1977. Music is a special system of sounds that can transmit emotions. The sounds have certain structure, pitches, durations, and tone. These features can be examined by a computer with an ad hoc software system. Then the recognized features can be translated into a special notation system such as a score or MIDI notations for electric instruments. This method is the musical transcription.

In this thesis the base of a later music information system have been developed in MATLAB, the popular technical computing language and environment. The developed programs cover many fields of musical transcription. Frequency detection, note detection, chord detection, and beat detection algorithms have been worked out as MATLAB programs. Each of them is in an early state, but they are capable of recognize features of real musical recordings. They can be the base of a future music information system with further development.

The worked out methods differs from the existing ones that available on various papers of existing literature. This thesis takes the musical aspects mostly of the various transcription problems.

Keywords: Musical transcription, Frequency detection, Note detection, Chord detection, Beat detection, Discrete Fourier Transform, Fast Fourier Transform.

Chapter 1

Basics of Music

The problem of music analysis can be difficult. First of all we have to find certain features to examine. Songs may have repeated parts such as chorus or verses. Other key feature can be the melody or chords that form the basis of the song. If we have human voice (singing in most cases) we can analyze it separately. The smallest components of songs are notes, and they have other features, like pitch or duration. Other feature is that what kind of instruments take part in the music. Before we go into structural analysis of music, here come some basic things we have to make clear.

1.1 Instruments and lyrics in songs

Music is quintessentially a mixture of instruments and vocals in most cases. Musicians play the instruments to sound a certain melody. They often have some pieces of paper called sheet music. Nowadays it is used mostly in classical music. The sheet music has a kind of structure that reflects the thoughts of composers. Figure 1.1 shows a short part of a sheet music. It has notes (musical notation signs) that show the pitch and the duration of the note among other things. The score is the book form of sheet music, it usually has musical notations for all the instruments in a song. The structure of the score has an effect on the structure of music. Popular music also has this structure but it is partly came from lyrics. Lyrics form other structural elements: verses, bridges, choruses.

Figure 1.1: *Example of a sheet music*

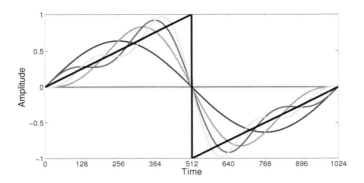

Figure 1.2: *Decomposition of a sawtooth wave*

1.2   Properties of sound

If we hear a sound we can observe some properties of it. It has a certain loudness, pitch and a unique tone. Basically the sound travels as a wave in the air. This wave goes into the ears and makes the eardrums vibrate. We can describe this wave as a time function. The most obvious way to measure it is using a microphone connected to an oscilloscope. The signal appears on the screen is proportional to the waveform of the observed sound. There are certain relations between the waveform and the properties of the sound. The loudness depends on the amplitude of the wave and the pitch depends on frequency. Bigger amplitude means louder sound while bigger frequency means higher sound. The relation between them is logarithmic because of the logarithmic property of ears. The tone comes from the shape of the wave. The simplest shape is a sinusoidal curve and every periodic signal can describe as a constant member plus a linear combination of different sinusoids called harmonics. The sinusoid has the lowest frequency (first harmonic) is the fundamental frequency, the others are the overtones, they are integer multiples of the fundamental frequency. The first harmonic gives the pitch, the distribution and intensity of the rest gives the timbre or tone. Figure 1.2 shows a sawtooth wave composed with 1,2,3,4 and infinite sinusoidal components and a constant member. This kind of decomposition is called Fourier Transform [2]. The Fourier Transform is a very useful tool to transform signals from time domain to frequency domain.

1.3   Notes

We won't go into details of notes, but we have to know about some basic properties of them. In music, musicians and singers use special frequencies that represent fixed pitches called notes. The graphic representation of these pitches on music sheet are also called notes. For the sake of easy notation these notes have simple names. The names are these letters: **A,B,C,D,E,F,G** in order of rising pitch

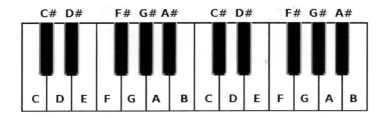

Figure 1.3: *Notes on a piano keyboard, two octaves*

(**B** is **H** in some languages, like German or Hungarian). Note **A** has a standardized frequency, it is 440 Hz. These letter names are repeated, so **A** follows **G** an octave higher than the first **A**. An octave means double frequency (more precisely, the interval between two frequencies having a ratio 2 to 1), so this **A** has 880 Hz frequency while the **A** two octaves lower is 220 Hz. We can use a special suffix notation to show which octave the note falls in. **A4** means **A** with 440 Hz, **A3** means 220 Hz, **A5** means 880 Hz. In music 12 notes exist in an octave, but we have only 7 names. Take a closer look at the piano keyboard on Figure 1.3, we can observe white and black keys. The white keys represent **A,B,C,D,E,F,G** while black ones has # suffix in their names. The distance between notes and its pairs notated with # is a semitone. Note **E,F** and **B,C** don't have any additional notes between them, each pair has a semitone distance between their members. Some definitions mention note as a distance, it would be the distance between white keys in our case. Consider an octave, we have 12 notes, every octaves starts with **C**: **C,C#,D,D#,E,F,F#,G,G#,A,A#,B**.

note	octave 2	octave 3	octave 4	octave 5	octave 6
C	65.4064	130.8128	261.6256	523.2511	1046.5022
C#	69.2957	138.5913	277.1826	554.3653	1108.7306
D	73.4162	146.8324	293.6648	587.3295	1174.6590
D#	77.7817	155.5635	311.1270	622.2540	1244.5080
E	82.4069	164.8138	329.6276	659.2551	1318.5102
F	87.3071	174.6141	349.2282	698.4565	1396.9130
F#	92.4986	184.9972	369.9944	739.9888	1479.9776
G	97.9989	195.9977	391.9954	783.9909	1567.9818
G#	103.8262	207.6523	415.3047	830.6094	1661.2188
A	110.0000	220.0000	**440.0000**	880.0000	1760.0000
A#	116.5409	233.0819	466.1638	932.3275	1864.6550
B	123.4708	246.9417	493.8833	987.7666	1975.5332

Table 1.1: *Frequencies from C2 to B6 in Hertz*

What are their frequencies? **C** follows **B** in an octave higher, it has the double frequency of the first **C**. There are 12 notes between the two frequencies so we have to compute the twelfth root of two:

$$m = \sqrt[12]{2} \tag{1.1}$$

And now we can compute the frequencies easily if we have a base note. Computing the neighboring notes are simply multiplying and dividing by m. Consider we like to know the frequency of **G#4** and **A#4**. Both have a semitone distance from **A4** and we know its frequency is 440 Hz. **G#4** is a semitone below **A4** so we have to divide 440 Hz with m and **A#4** is a semitone above, we have to multiply:

$$f_{G\#4} = f_{A4}/m = 440\,Hz/\sqrt[12]{2} = 415.3047\,Hz \tag{1.2}$$
$$f_{A\#4} = f_{A4}m = 440\,Hz\,\sqrt[12]{2} = 466.1638\,Hz$$

So we can compute every frequency from 440Hz, using the method described in Equation 1.2. The methods of this thesis are implemented in MATLAB (Programming Language for Technical Computing, see [2]). Here is a short algorithm in MATLAB, that calculates the frequencies of notes from **C2** to **B6** (part of *generate_notes.m*, see Appendix):

```
bottom=1;              %  1 ~ C2
top=60;                % 60 ~ B6

notes = [];
next_note_m = 2^(1/12);
%%% Note A4 is 440 Hz
note_a = 440;

sh = note_a;
%%% Compute the notes above 440 Hz
for k = 34:top
    notes(k) = sh;
    sh = sh * next_note_m;
end

sh = note_a;

%%% Compute the notes below 440 Hz
for k = 33:-1:bottom
    sh = sh / next_note_m;
    notes(k) = sh;
end
```

Then vector *notes* will contain the frequencies from **C2** to **B6**. These frequencies will be important for us, Table 1.1 shows them. These are the most used frequencies in melodies, lower notes are used mostly for bass accompaniment. The note range of an ordinary six-string guitar is about from **C3** to **E7** depends on tuning. The range of a standard piano with 88 keys is from **A0** to **C8**.

1.4 Chords

1.4.1 Basics of chords

In music and music theory, a chord is three or more different notes or pitches sounding simultaneously, or nearly simultaneously, over a period of time. Every chord is given a specific name, based on the notes that constitute the chord and the distances, or intervals, between them. The simplest and possibly most frequently used chords are trichords, meaning they have three ("tri") notes (before any doubling of notes, that is), four notes form a tetrachord, six a hexachord, etc [3].

1.4.2 The triads

The most commonly used chords in popular music, the triads are a kind of trichord. They are composed of three notes: a root note, a note which is a third above the root, and a note which is a third above that note, and therefore a fifth above the root. Each note has a function within the chord: the note the chord is built on is called the *root* of the chord, the second note (a third above the root) is called the *third* of the chord, and the third note (a third above the second note) is called the *fifth* of the chord. There are two main types of triads: major and minor. For example C,E,G is a triad together, the root note is **C**, the third of the root is **E**, the fifth above the root is **G**. The major triads have a 1-5-8 construction in semitones where 1 is **C**, 2 is **C#** and so on. This chord called C major, where C indicates the root note, and major is the type of the chord. Minor triads has 1-4-8 construction. That is, now we can construct two types of chord on a note. Consider **G** as the root note, and 1-5-8 construction where 1 is **G**. Then we obtain the third of the root is **B** and the fifth is **D**. This chord is G major. G minor is almost the same, the difference is the third of the root, it is **A#**. Figure 1.4 shows a C major and Figure 1.5 a G minor chord. As it seen in the figures, any of the notes can repeat themselves in an other octave or any of the notes can be in an other octave than the others. Major and minor triads are the most important chords in popular music. They form the basis of many pop songs that means the melody comes from them. Musicians play the chords one after the other and use the notes in chords to play solos or sing the lyrics of the song. Of course, major and minor triads are not enough for all genre of music, other types of chords are required.

- notations (with root note **C**):

  - Major triads: simply the root note name, C

  - Minor triads: root name and letter 'm', Cm

5

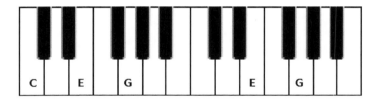

Figure 1.4: *A C major chord*

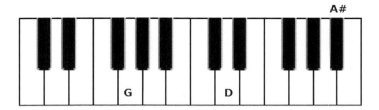

Figure 1.5: *A G minor chord*

1.4.3   Seventh chords

Seventh chords are constructed by adding a fourth note to a triad, at the interval of a third above the fifth of the chord. This creates the interval of a seventh above the root of the chord. There are various types of seventh chords depending on the type of the original triad chord and the added seventh note. There are simple and minor seventh chord, according to the type of the original triad. The notes in simple seventh chord has 1-5-8-11 construction in semitones, and 1-4-8-11 in minor seventh chord. Major seventh chord differs in the fourth note, it is a semitone above than in simple seventh, so the notes have 1-5-8-12 construction.

- notations:

    - Simple seventh: root name and '7', C7

    - Minor seventh: root name and 'm7', Cm7

    - Major seventh: root name and 'maj7', Cmaj7

1.4.4   Extended chords

Extended chords are triads with notes added beyond the seventh. Thus ninth, eleventh, and thirteenth chords are extended chords.

- notations:

  - Ninth chords: root name and '9', C9

  - Eleventh chords: root name and '11', C11

  - Thirteenth chords: root name and '13', C13

1.4.5 Sustained chords

A sustained chord, or "sus chord" (also suspended chord), is a chord where the second or most often the fourth is played with or replaces the third. For instance, the chord noted Csus4 is **C**,**F**, and **G**.

- notations:

  - Simple sustained: root name and 'sus4', Csus4

  - Sustained with seventh: root name and '7sus4', C7sus4

1.4.6 Sixth chords

Sixth chords are very similar to seventh chords except the fourth note, it is six above the root in notes (ten in semitones). There are two main types of them, major and minor according to the base triad.

- notations:

  - Major sixth: root name and '6', C6

  - Minor sixth: root name and 'm6', Cm6

1.4.7 Other types of chords

These were the most important and most played chords. There are other types of chords, some of them are a certain kind of mixture of the above-mentioned chords. We will mention them later in Chapter 4, where a database of chords will be built.

1.4.8 Example

Here is an example, a part of a song from Pink Floyd called "Wish you were Here" [1]:

```
(intro part)

Em   /   G   /   Em   /   G  /  Em   /  Am7  /  Em   /
Am7  /   G   /   G
```

```
C                                  D                    Am
   So, so you think you can tell, heaven from hell?
                         G
   Blue skies from pain?


                           D                        C
   Can you tell a green field, from a cold steel rail?
                    Am
   A smile from a veil?


                         G                        C
   Do you think you can tell?  Did they get you to trade,
                       D
   your heroes for ghost


   . . .
```

This was the first rows of the lyrics, noted the chords above the text. The intro part contains some seventh chords, the others are simple minor and major chords. The used chords are C,D,G,Am in the rest of the song.

Chapter 2

Existing tools for music transcription

This chapter is a literature review of existing tools.

2.1 Transcription

Musical transcription of audio data is the process of taking a sequence of digital data corresponding to the sound waveform and extracting the symbolic information related to the high-level musical structures [7]. The transcription result is typically given in the form of a musical notation which comprises the times, durations, and pitches of the sounds [23]. The transcription can divide into two parts: pitch (or note) and beat detection. Pitch detection has further two parts, monophonic and polyphonic. Monophonic pitch detection deals with one instrument recognition, polyphonic detection means the real-world music analysis with several instruments.

2.1.1 History of transcription evolution

Here is a historical overview of transcription till early 90's [26]. Transcription traces back to two papers. One paper is by Straszczalki and the other by Moorer from Stanford, both in the first edition of the Computer Music Journal in 1977. Moorer predates Straszczalki with his 1975 doctoral thesis at Stanford. Moorer's initial doctoral thesis begins by attempting tackle the problem polyphonic music directly. Moorer generalized his initial findings to any two monophonic instruments. There were severe restrictions, however, on what the instruments could play. No overlap was permitted between the notes, or any harmonics of the notes. Beat detection was added as an afterthought by requiring the user to input the minimum beat of the piece. The rest of the durations were mapped as a multiples of this value [28]. Piszczalski's initial paper in 1977 was specific to monophonic recorder or symphonic flute - both instruments that have particularly strong fundamental frequencies. Piszczalski first converted the signal to the frequency domain, then chose the most dominant partial as the fundamental frequency. Similar to Moorer, the smallest duration is provided by the user and used to calculate the duration of all remaining notes [30]. Piszczalski's follow up paper with Galler, Bossemeyer, and Looft in 1981 extended this work to arbitrary harmonic instruments, but maintained the same basic algorithm used in the original 1977 paper [29]. Foster, Schloss, and Rockmore took a very different approach in their 1982 paper. They noted that amplitude thresholding has serious limitations in detecting notes, so they utilized autoregressive techniques for detecting note boundaries [15]. Chafe, Mont-Reynaud, and Rush wrote the first higher level processor. It built upon Foster's note detection algorithm. Their algorithm was able to detect some kind of duration [9]. In 1983 Lerdhal and Jackenoff wrote a book, General Theory of Tonal Music. It described a serious of rules for grouping and inferring meter (the term meter will be explained later). This book became the foundation of most of the transcription work that followed [24]. Mount-Reynaud published a pattern matching algorithm in 1985 while he was working on a very different approach with Chafe, Jaffe Kashima and Smith in the same year. In their algorithm music is processed repeatedly using a blackboard algorithm. In addition, they use a BoundedQ frequency analysis instead of a transform from the DFT (see Section 3.2) family [8]. Desian and Honings' 1989 paper on quantization of musical time marks the first paper explicitly on beat tracking [11]. Kashino and Tanaka's approach was different, they began by extracting frequency components. Partials were then clustered by timbre theory, forming notes. Notes were then assigned to sound sources in a second stage of clustering [21]. By early 90's, there was an explosion of papers on various different areas of transcription, but it is still an open problem.

2.1.2   Monophonic pitch recognition

The main problem of the pitch recognition appears when we transform the sound signal to frequency domain. Because the FFT results are linearly spaced, higher notes will be more widely separated in frequency than lower notes (see Table 1.1 on page 3). It means it is harder to detect low frequency notes than higher notes. Maher gave an example of this using the sequence of frequency components 110, 220, 330, and 440Hz [10]. If a 2Hz resolution was used, the sequence could be measured as 108, 222, 328, and 442Hz. If 108Hz was chosen as the fundamental frequency, then the predicted sequence would be 108, 216, 324, 432Hz. The difference between the predicted sequence and the badly measured sequence is 0, 6, 4, 10Hz. With the correct fundamental frequency the difference sequence would be 2, 2, 2, 2Hz. The best predicted sequence is found when the sum of the difference sequence is a minimum. Monti and Dandle [27] described a monophonic transcription with autocorrelation. They chose autocorrelation pitch tracking to estimate the pitch in the musical signal. The interesting part of a note is the steady part. The steady part of a note is just after the attack when all the harmonics become stable and clearly marked in the spectrum. They gave the autocorrelation equation in time domain. N is the length of the sequence noted $x(k)$:

$$r_{xx}(n) = \frac{1}{N} \sum_{k=0}^{N-n-1} x(k) * x(k+n) \tag{2.1}$$

Where n is the lag, or the period length, and $x(n)$ is the time domain signal. Peaks in the autocorrelation function correspond to the lags where periodicity is stronger. The zero lag autocorrelation function $r_{xx}(0)$ is the energy of the signal. The first peak in the autocorrelation is the inverse of fundamental frequency, while the other values discarded. The calculation of the autocorrelation is computed through FFT, which has a computational complexity of $N \cdot log(N)$, where N is the length of the windowed signal. The calculation process is therefore very fast. So autocorrelation is simple, fast, and reliable. However, it is useless itself on polyphonic signals.

2.1.3 Polyphonic pitch detection

The problem of polyphonic pitch detection comes from the several different sounds at the same time. They may have common harmonics, even if their fundamental frequencies are different. The pitch detection of harmonics is not enough in general, high-level recognition is recommended. That means the detection algorithm has to have the capability to "understand" music not only "hear" it. Several methods have been developed over the years.

Piano recordings

Some methods are specially developed for piano recordings.

Paper [6] describes a temporal segmentation algorithm. This system divides the piano piece into temporal slots and, afterwards, a frequency analysis of each slot is done. Each temporal slot starts when a new onset is detected that means when a new note is played. This type of temporal segmentation is very well suited for the frequency analysis because new frequencies appear in the music signal when a new note is played. Onset detection is realized in time domain with a sliding window on the energy signal calculated as the square of the signal. Then comes a frequency analysis that determines which of the notes were played in the current attack (current slot) and which are due to previous attacks. The algorithm can estimate the beat from the length of detected notes. Marolt [25] applied machine learned algorithms in musical transcription limited to transcription of polyphonic piano music. He used neural network models with adaptive networks of coupled adaptive oscillators to improve transcription accuracy and robustness. Dixon [12] used downsampling to 12 kHz, then applied FFT window of 4096 samples (341ms), containing 230ms of signal shaped by a Hamming window and zero padded to fill the window. The size and shape of the window can be changed by command line parameters. He used overlapped windows for more accuracy. See [35] or Chapter 3 for explanations of window shapes and overlapped windows. Abdallah and Plumbley's [4] system is based on probabilistic model equivalent to a form of noisy independent component analysis (ICA) or sparse coding with non-negativity constraints.

General music

Fundamentally, music consists of sounds generated concurrently by a number of different sources (usually musical instruments of varying kinds) [19]. These sources generally fall into two categories: harmonic and percussive. Harmonic sounds forms notes with its harmonic components. Percussive sounds, on the other hand, lack harmonic structure and are more analogous to noise clouds. Drums and cymbals are the obvious examples of this class. Transcription of polyphonic music introduces

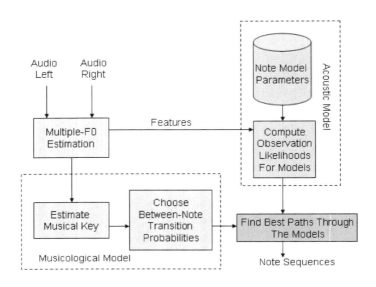

Figure 2.1: *The block diagram of the transcription method in [33]*

a number of new complexities that are not present in the monophonic version of this problem [31]. Since we have more than one possible note at once, we can no longer be sure that there is a single delay at which the whole waveform will repeat, so the autocorrelation approach is no suitable. We have to identify the frequency components (harmonics) corresponding to each individual notes, including fundamental frequency and the multiples of them. Unfortunately, in most cases some of the detected harmonics can be the part of two or more different notes. Here is a complex method of polyphonic music transcription from Ryynänen and Klapuri [33] described on Figure 2.1. The method based on Klapuri's other papers, including one from 2001 [22]. They proposed differentiating the logarithm of the amplitude envelopes at each band. In this case, oscillations in the amplitude envelope do not matter too much after the sound has set on. This way makes easier the detection onsets, the start points of notes. Multipitch estimation forms the core of their transcription. They used an iterative succession, as it illustrated on Figure 2.2. One step of the iteration removes the detected sound due to the next step. The first part predominant pitch estimation, refers to the crucial stage where the pitch of the most prominent sound is estimated in the interference of other harmonic and noisy sounds. This is achieved by utilizing the harmonic concordance of simultaneous spectral components. In the second part, the spectrum of the detected sound is estimated and linearly subtracted from the mixture. The estimation and subtraction steps are then repeated for the residual signal. There is interesting audible examples in MP3 on Matti Ryynänen's demos page [32]. Gribonval and Bacry used harmonic and Gabor atoms [18] instead of plain FFT. They introduced many kind of matching pursuit algorithms with

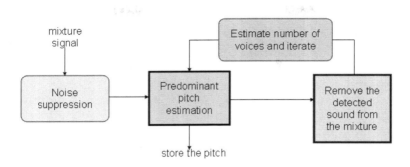

Figure 2.2: *The iteration part of the multipitch estimation algorithm [22]*

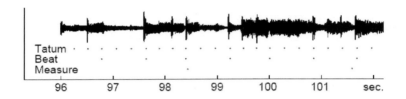

Figure 2.3: *Metrical levels of a recording [23]*

complex mathematical theory to detect notes even in difficult situations. Heinsworth and his company published a paper about analysis of reassigned spectrograms that can help in music transcription [20]. The reassignment method for the short-time Fourier transform is proposed as a technique for improving the time and frequency estimates of musical audio data. Based on this representation, four classes of expected objects (sinusoid, unresolved sinusoid, transient and noise) are proposed and explained. The main benefits of the proposed reassignment stage are that it yields an improved time-frequency localization estimate relative to standard methods, and that it produces a measure of the variance of these estimates to be used as an aid in later processing. Ellis wrote an interesting summary of transcription using slides with many figures and explanations [13].

2.1.4 Meter detection

Klapuri has a good paper that explains meter estimation [23]. Musical signals exhibit temporal regularity, a meter. Perceiving musical meter can be characterized as processing musical events so that underlying periodicities are detected. Musical meter is hierarchical in structure, consisting of pulse sensations at different levels, see Figure 2.3.

The most prominent metrical level is beat (foot tapping rate). Tatum (time quantum) refers to the shortest duration values in music that are still more than incidentally encountered. The other duration values with few exceptions, are integer multiples of the tatum. Klapuri detected changes in power intensity, used a bank of comb-filter resonators, then applied a probabilistic model for meter estimation. A paper from Princeton deals with discrete wavelet transform (DWT) [36]. The signal is first decomposed into a number of octave frequency bands using the DWT in this method. After that the time domain amplitude envelope of each band is extracted separately. This is achieved by low pass filtering each band, applying full wave rectification and downsampling. The envelopes of each band are then summed together and an autocorrelation function is computed. The peaks of the autocorrelation function correspond to the various periodicities of the signal's envelope. Scheirer introduced a method using a small number of bandpass filters and banks of parallel comb filters to analyze the tempo of, and extract the beat from, musical signals of arbitrary polyphonic complexity and containing arbitrary timbres [34]. This analysis is performed causally, and can be used predictively to guess when beats occur in the future.

Goto and Muraoka developed a method for drumless audio signals, it is looking for chord changes to estimate the beat [17].

2.2 The aim of transcription

The sense of transcription is very obvious: convert any recorded music from any type of media to special notation systems such as MIDI data, sheet music, or score. Recognizing and naming of heard notes and chords are very difficult even for musicians. Automatic transcription can help in this case. A transcription program would be of use to musicologists researching the large corpus of recorded music for whom a score would be an invaluable aid. Imagine a computer that is able to be an accompanist of a musician! It could be possible with automatic transcription. A commercial application is to make ringtones for mobile phones from our favorite songs. Other commercial application is to make scores for any music that doesn't have one. In research, process music with computers has led to a greater understanding of the underlying principles of music.

2.3 Application fields

2.3.1 MIDI

The result of the musical transcription, the high-level musical structure can be MIDI notations. Musical Instruments Digital Interface, or MIDI, is an industry-standard electronic communications protocol that defines each musical note in an electronic musical instrument such as a synthesizer, precisely and concisely, allowing electronic musical instruments and computers to exchange data, or "talk", with each other. MIDI does not transmit audio - it simply transmits digital information about a music performance [3]. When a note is played by a musician, the musical instrument send a MIDI message.

This example shows what type of MIDI messages are generated when a key being struck and released on a synthesizer keyboard:

1. the user started playing a **C** note, with the specified velocity (volume)

2. the user changed the force with which he is holding the key down (can be repeated, optional)

3. the user stopped playing the **C** note

Note messages can represent any note from **C** with 8.175 Hz (it could be **C-1**, but **A0** is the lowest note on most piano keyboards) to **G** with 12557 Hz (**G9**, this is also not a real note). **C-1** designated as MIDI note 0, and **G9** as MIDI note 127 and of course the precision is a semitone. Therefore MIDI note 69 is equal to **A4**. MIDI messages (along with timing information) can be collected and stored in a computer file system, in what is commonly called a MIDI file.

2.3.2 Audio to MIDI converter tools

Johann Forsberg wrote a thesis about sound converting to MIDI format based on constant Q transform [14]. Moreover, there already exist some software that can convert audio to MIDI files. MuseBook WAV to MIDI converts monophonic (44.1 KHz 16 bit mono) Wave file into MIDI file. It analyzes Wave file, detects pitch, onset and timbre of sound and produces a MIDI file. The pitch bandwidth is from **A0** to **C8**, that equals to pianos with 88 keys. Time resolution is 11 msec (http://www.musebook.com/?page=mbwav2midi).

Widisofts' WIDI Recognition System can convert WAV and MP3 files to MIDI files. It can process polyphonic music both in real-time and off-line mode. In real-time mode, this software can instantly convert music from the microphone or line input of a computer into a MIDI sequence (http://www.widisoft.com).

Akoff Sound Labs developed several music tools including AKoff Music Composer. It has polyphonic music recognition from pre-recorded WAVE files or directly from audio input of a sound card in real-time, using different harmonic models to improve recognition (http://www.akoff.com/music-composer.html).

Araki Software has an interesting tool. AmazingMIDI automatically transcribes music, it can recognize single-instrument polyphonic music. The output is a MIDI file, and it has two inputs: an Input File, and a Tone File. AmazingMIDI analyzes the Input File, assuming that every sound in the file is played with the same tone color as the one in the Tone File. As a result, even if the music contains several different instruments, AmazingMIDI writes down all detected notes as a single-instrument music. AmazingMIDI is freeware from 2003 (http://www.pluto.dti.ne.jp/ araki/amazingmidi/).

Tallstick Sound Project has a polyphonic recognition software with simple and user-friendly interface called TS-AudioToMIDI. It has some special features: manual and auto tuning to correct possible audio signal frequency deviation from the standard note frequencies; sensor selectivity and sharpness controls with graphic representation; Graphic Harmonic Model control, setting up first four harmonics of recognized instrument (http://audioto.com/eng/aud2midi.htm).

However, these are commercial softwares (except of AmazingMIDI), and therefore we can't find out the algorithms the programs built on. They require Windows operation system, so using them on other platforms is very hard. Free downloads are available with restrictions on some capabilities, like saving MIDI files. There are a dozen MIDI softwares for UNIX and Linux systems such as sequencers, players, utilities, environments. Of course, they are free softwares and their source code is also available and commutable. Unfortunately there is not any kind of audio to MIDI converter software according to linux-sound.org and the available packages of the Debian distribution (in 2005).

Chapter 3

Note detection

In this chapter a simple but efficient algorithm will be constructed to detect notes. It works only with monophonic sound, that means only one note is permitted in a period of time. Although it will be a note detection algorithm, the duration won't be calculated (it can be estimated from window sizes), the pitch will be matched to the frequencies of notes.

3.1 Handle of music recordings

Recorded music on CDs has a standard refers to their record format. Because of CD is a digital medium, the sound wave is stored in a digital form. It has finite samples both in time and amplitude. The number of the samples are 44100 in a second, because the maximal recorded frequency is 22050 Hz. A sample point has 65536 intensity levels from 0 to 65535, it is exactly the values we can represent on two bytes. Stereo music requires 2 independent channels. After a short calculation, we get 176400 bytes in a second that can reproduce the recorded music in a quite well quality. This standard is the CD quality. On a computer file system, this record is realized as a wave file contains exactly the same played bytes as on CD. x86 architectures have a standard wave file format with .wav extension, independently of the operation system. In MATLAB, special functions (*wavread.m* and *wavwrite.m*) can convert a wave file into a single vector and vice versa. *Wawread.m* reads a wave file into a vector. In case of stereo wave file, the vector has two columns. New function was written to handle stereo files, *wavload.m*. It treats stereo recordings as a simple mono wave, the wave is the average of left and right channels.

The most popular and widely used music file format is MP3. MP3 is the compact format of music records, the MP3 file size is 5-12 times shorter than WAV files. However, the sound quality of MP3 is poorer compared to CD quality.

3.2 Fourier Transform

In our aspect the Fourier Transform can translate our sound wave from time domain into frequency domain.

There is a special kind of Fourier Transform for discrete values called Discrete Fourier Transform (DFT). The base equation of the DFT for time function f with N points [35]:

$$D(n) = \frac{1}{N} \sum_{i=0}^{N-1} f(i) e^{-j \frac{2\pi}{N} in} \qquad 0 \leq n \leq N - 1 \tag{3.1}$$

D is the transformed vector in frequency domain. As it seen on (3.1), D has the same number of elements as f. The elements of D are complex numbers, even if f is real. The absolute value of the elements in D give the amplitudes of the frequency components, the angles of the complex numbers give the phases for each frequency component. In practice, calculation with this equation takes a long time. Consider we have 8192 sample points, the number of multiplications and additions would be 8192·8192 ($N \cdot N$), that is 67,108,864 (over 67 million operations). There is an algorithm based on (3.1) called Fast Fourier Transform, FFT. The mathematical part of FFT is fundamentally the same as in DFT, the calculating method differs. The number of operations is only $log_2 N \cdot N$, with 8192 sample points 13·8192=106,496 (630 times faster in this case). The only restriction is that N must be a power of 2.

If the input vector is real, $D(0)$ and $D(N/2)$ will be also real, and we can ignore the second half of the output, so $D(0), D(1), D(2), ..., D(N/2 - 1), D(N/2)$ unequivocally determine the transform of the N-sized real input vector[35].

3.3 FFT on sound data

We apply the FFT on a real song 'Things Like This'. See Appendix for details. The song is piano based with singing and strings that come later. The first three notes played on the piano are **A5 B5 C6**. When key **C6** is attacked, the musician starts to accompany the melody with his left hand, so other notes are played simultaneously some octaves below. We will focus on the first two notes. Figure 3.1 shows the wave form of this two notes. The time is represented in sample points, the amplitude is normalized between -1 and 1. We work with one wave, stereo records are reduced to one channel (left, right, or the average of them in our case). The length of the first note **A5** is approximately 8000 sample points, it is more than 0.18 seconds a little bit, the sample has 44100 points in a second. Consider we want to analyze this first note with FFT. It is obvious to apply the FFT on the first 8000 points, but the FFT requires the number of points to be power of two. When we apply the FFT on 8192 points, the result has also 8192 elements, 8192 complex numbers. The second half of the result vector is the reflection of the first half, because the input vector was real [35], so we can ignore it. The length of the interesting first part is 4096 because we compute the FFT on 8192 points, and we have 44100 points in a second, the resolution is 44100 Hz/8192 = 5.3833 Hz. According to Shannon's theory [2] the maximal sound frequency we can represent is 22050 Hz with 44100 Hz sampling frequency. We have

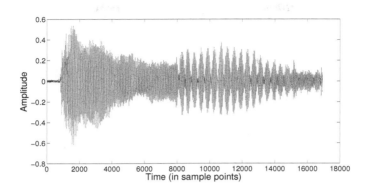

Figure 3.1: *Wave form of the first two notes of 'Things Like This'*

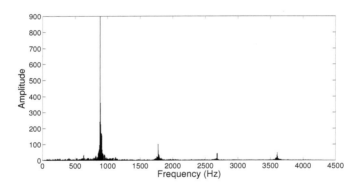

Figure 3.2: *The FFT of the first note in 'Things Like This'*

4096 transformed values, the distances are 5.3833 Hz between each of them. The first value tells the properties (amplitude and phase) of the 5.3833 Hz component, the second corresponds to 10.7666 Hz, the last 4096th value is about the 22050 Hz component. So the result vector is linearly separated from 5.3833 Hz to 22050 Hz, the resolution is 5.3833 Hz. The 0th element, '0 Hz' is a special case. It is the constant member, with Equation 3.1 it is computed automatically (it is the average of the signal when $n = 0$). In MATLAB's FFT function the constant member is the first element of the result vector which is confusing sometimes. The FFT of the first note **A5** is shown in Figure 3.2. The first peak is the fundamental frequency, it is around 880 Hz as we expected (see Table 1.1 on page 3). We have to face a problem, we don't have 880 Hz in our frequency spectrum! The 163rd point represents 877.48 Hz while the 164th point represents 882.86 Hz. We are not able to detect the proper frequency of the first peak, either it is 880 Hz or differs from 880 Hz a little bit.

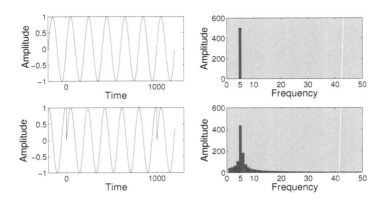

Figure 3.3: *'Finite window problem' with a 5 Hz signal (top) and a 5.3 Hz (bottom)*

3.4 The problem of finite window with DFT

The DFT is designed for periodic signals. When we choose a finite sequence of data in a window, we don't care about the signal before and after the window. It leads to problem, because the DFT considers the signal as a periodic signal and assumes that the data is repeated continuously outside the window. Consider x is the input vector, N is the length of the window, then the DFT assumes that $x(i + N) = x(i)$. The result of this problem is in Figure 3.3 for a window of 1000 points. The top of the figure shows the very rare case with real-world data, it is when the window size is integer multiple of the periodic time of the signal. We get false spectra mostly, as it is shown at the bottom. However, we can take the advantage of this error to correct our detection. The solutions of finite window problem are the various window functions, Hanning and Hamming windows (see [2] or [35]) are the most used. For the sake of accuracy, we won't use any of them in frequency detection.

3.5 More precise frequency detection with its represented neighbors

Consider y_1 and y_2 the values of neighboring represented frequencies noted x_1 and x_2 in the transformed spectrum. All we know, we have only one peak that is much more higher than its surroundings. If it is between x_1 and x_2, both of them will have a peak. In our case, the expected peak on 880 Hz has an effect both on the represented 877.48 and 882.86 Hz slot. It is simply conceivable that a 877.48 Hz signal would cause a peak in the 163rd point and would have no effect on the 164th point. A signal between exactly the two frequencies causes that the two slots will have (almost) the same peak.

$$x = x_1 + \frac{y_2}{y_1 + y_2} r = x_2 - \frac{y_1}{y_1 + y_2} r \qquad r = x_2 - x_1 \qquad (3.2)$$

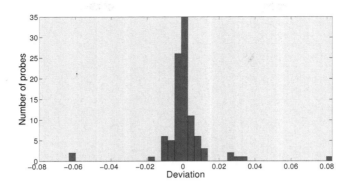

Figure 3.4: *Deviations of 100 detected random frequencies (20-2000 Hz)*

Where x is the detected frequency. That is, we get generally frequency peaks in pairs in the spectrum and we can estimate the correct frequency from both of them. Equation 3.2 can be computed fast and the accuracy of the results are very impressive as it is seen in Figure 3.4. 100 tests were executed to check the accuracy. Each test generated a random sinusoid with random frequency and phase. The maximum of the random frequencies were 2000 Hz, according to the last note in our frequency table (Table 1.1 page 3). The size of the sinusoids were 44100 points, the window size of the FFT was 8192. The generality of the deviation values are less than 0.02 Hz, and all of them less than 0.1 Hz. It means 0.1 Hz accuracy in the worst case in contrast with 5.3833 Hz (calculate these tests with Hamming window, the maximal deviation grows to 1.6 Hz, with Hanning window it is 1.8 Hz). With higher frequencies (more than 2000 Hz) the accuracy grows, for random frequencies between 10000 and 20000 Hz the maximum deviation was only **0.0015 Hz** with the same test method (*deviation.m* was developed for the tests).

Back to 'Things Like This', we will compute the frequency of the first note. We have to find the maximum peak in the spectrum, and that is in slot 163. We put 0 into this slot and find the next maximum, it will be in frequency slot 164. With Equation 3.2 the calculated frequency is **879.9969 Hz**. The MATLAB function *find_freq.m* was developed for the above-mentioned frequency calculation method (see Appendix).

3.6 Note detection with frequency mapping

Many ranges of the frequency domain should not be detected as a note. According to Table 1.1, we should care about only some frequency slots. We have to map the interesting frequency pairs from the spectrum to a vector that represents the notes. Here is the algorithm of mapping (*translate_notes.m*):

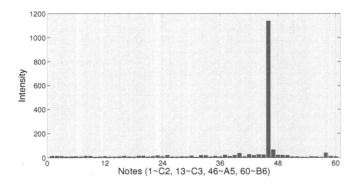

Figure 3.5: *Intensity of notes when key A5 is attacked*

```
window = 8192;
wt = window/44100;
wscale = wt*notes;
mapped_notes = [];
for k = 1:length(wscale)
    mapped_notes = [mapped_notes; ...
                    fix(wscale(k)) fix(wscale(k))+1];
end
```

Vector *notes* comes from *generate_notes.m* (see on page 4), it contains the frequencies of notes we want to detect. Result vector *mapped_notes* has exactly the same size as *notes*. The elements of *mapped_notes* are numerical pairs, each pair represents a note and each pair is an index in the frequency domain of our spectrum. The explanation of pairs are the same as it was described in Section 3.5. For example, the index of **A4** is (81,82), index of **A5** is (163,164). We choose frequency slots from the spectrum according to the pairs in *mapped_notes* and generate an intensity level for each note. With this method, we calculate one intensity level from two neighboring values. We can apply a simple addition, like this: $i_{A5} = s(163) + s(164)$, where s is the spectrum (see Figure 3.2). It guarantees that we get a peak in case of 880 Hz, that causes a peak both in frequency slot 163 and 164. Figure 3.5 shows the calculated intensities of notes. The only thing we have to investigate is the place of the maximal value in this mapped spectrum.

C3	C#3	D3	D#3	E3	F3	F#3	G3	G#3	A3	A#3	B3
24	25	27	28	30	32	34	36	38	40	43	45
25	26	28	29	31	33	35	37	39	41	44	46

Table 3.1: *Index of notes in octave 3 (when window size is 8192)*

Window size	First independent note	Time
1024	E6	23 msec
2048	E5	46 msec
4096	E4	93 msec
8192	E3	186 msec
16384	E2	372 msec

Table 3.2: *The first non-overlapped note with varied window sizes (in points and msec)*

3.7 Overlapped notes in mapping

Because of the resolution some of the lower notes are overlapped. The first pairs of *mapped_notes* are ((12,13),(12,13),(13,14),(14,15),(15,16),...). It means we can't separate notes, if we have a peak in lower ranges. If **C2** was played, **C#2** would also have a peak and **D2** would have a lower peak. The first non-overlapped pairs start from **E3** with this resolution. Table 3.1 shows the pairs in octave 3. (30,31) is the first non-overlapped pair, it belongs to **E3**. In practice, this is enough for analyze the sound of a guitar because its first string is tuned up to **E3** in general. However, most pianos have **A0** as the lowest key.

3.8 Time resolution versus frequency resolution

We chose window size 8192 arbitrary. It has a quite good resolution in frequency, but it can not be said for the time resolution. When time resolution is acceptable, the frequency resolution will be very low, see Figure 3.2. Even the shortest notes are not shorter than 100 ms in music [35]. The first note of 'Things Like This' takes approximate 180 ms in time, but in general we have to expect shorter notes. For general music analysis, 4096 window size is enough in time. The frequency resolution is around 11 Hz with this window.

3.9 Zero padding

Zero padding is a kind of cheat to improve frequency resolution. By zero-padding, the same window size is taken from the musical data, but it is then enlarged in length and filled, or padded, with zeros.

23

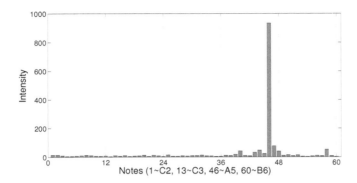

Figure 3.6: *Note A5 from 4096 samples padded to 16384 before FFT*

This does not reduce the time resolution because the same length windows are taken. However, the frequency resolution is increased because the window is larger before the FFT is applied [10].

The signal in this window differs from the original was taken from the music. It can be considered as a square function is multiplied with the data in the original window. The length of the square function is equal to the new window size, its value is 1 in the size of the old window, and then 0. The multiplication in time domain is convolution in frequency domain [2]. Therefore the spectrum of our signal will be convolved with an other spectrum.

Because of this convolution, we have to inspect the efficiency of zero padding. We use a 4096 original window size padded with zeros. The tests of random frequencies (described in section 3.5) results 2 Hz maximal deviation for 8192 size padded window. With 16384 size padded window it reduced to 1.27 Hz, and with 32768 window it is 0.7 Hz. With window size 65536, the maximal deviation stays around 0.6 Hz. It is enough to choose 16384 for the padded size of FFT window, or it can be bigger if we want to detect notes lower than **E2**. Figure 3.6 shows the first half of note **A5** in 'Things Like This' with 4096 original and 16384 padded windows. The figure is almost the same as Figure 3.5, the false frequency components stayed low.

3.10 Some errors that can affect note detection

3.10.1 Note change

Although we detect monophonic sound, the sound of **A5** is still ringing when key **B5** is attacked (the second note in 'Things Like This'), see Figure 3.7. This is not disturbing in most cases like ours, but we can design an algorithm that excepts the note we detected some windows before if it is necessary. The best idea is to trace the intensity level of a note. This can be done, if we apply the FFT continuously on the whole sound record. The intensity level has a peak when the note is started,

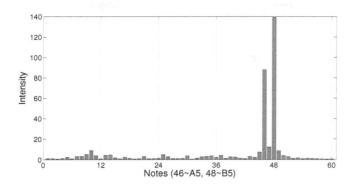

Figure 3.7: *Note B5 while A5 is still ringing*

then it has a sustained part with lower intensity, and fading in the end. Easier method is to detect the begins of notes (onsets) and after that don't care about the notes themselves. With this idea we won't be able to detect the exact duration of notes, the only thing left is the distance between notes in time. This note change checking won't be implemented in our algorithm.

3.10.2 Octave errors

As it was explained in Chapter 1, every tone has an individual wave form, that depends on the structure of harmonics. The frequency of the first harmonic is the fundamental frequency that determines the note, the other harmonics are the overtones. In Chapter 4 further interesting things will be presented about overtones. Overtones are also represented in the mapped spectra. If we take a closer look at Figure 3.6, we can see an overtone of **A5** in **A6** (the 58th bar on the figure). In general, they have lower intensity than their fundamental frequency. However, Figure 3.8 shows an interesting thing. It is the picked **A3** string of a guitar. The guitar was in a bad state, and it was directly connected to a computer microphone input, that caused the very poor quality. It seems like the fundamental frequency is **A2** and the first overtone is **A3** with higher intensity level than the fundamental frequency. In spite of this, the detected note will be the correct **A3** note. However, sometimes it occurs that the first overtone has larger peak than the fundamental frequency. In such cases, we have to check the same note an octave before. We examine the whole octave, whether it has a maximum peak. If the peak is exists, and the note is the same we detected an octave after, we correct the octave. For example, we change the detected note from **D4** to **D3**.

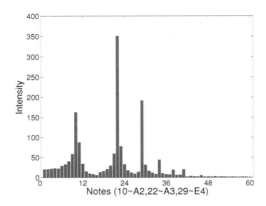

Figure 3.8: *String A3 on an electric guitar*

3.11   Monophonic transcription

The monophonic transcription can be taken with the above-mentioned note detection method. We simply take windows from the begin of the music record to the end, and applies the FFT on each window. Then we will have several mapped spectra, each of them corresponds to a certain time in the music. There is a technique that overlaps FFT windows, that means the FFT windows have common ranges. With zero padding, it is unnecessary. The end of a window is the begin of the next one (with no common point).

The song called 'Den Tunna Linjen' has the similar character in the beginning as 'Things Like This'. The first five seconds are played with two hands on the piano, but the number of lower notes are less than in 'Things Like This'. It is also not monophonic, but we can use our elementary transcription algorithm *(note_detection.m)*. In case of simultaneous notes we detect the stronger.

The MATLAB program *note_detection.m* contains *generate_notes.m* (see on page 4), *translate_notes.m* (see on page 22), and the indexing algorithm described in Section 3.6 *(frequency_index.m)*. The input is the wave file name, the original window size and the padded window size. In case of padded window size is equal to the original, no zero padding being applied. The outputs are nv, the sequence of the detected note names, $ns3d$ the sequence of indexed spectra, $nd3d$ is almost the same, the spectra contain only the detected notes. For the first part of 'Den Tunna Linjen', the result vector nv is this sequence:

A5 A5 A5 G5 G5 G5 G5 G5 D4 D4 D4 F#4 F#4 F#4 F#4 G5 G5 F#4...

The notes in octave 5 refers to the right hand of the musician, the others from octave 4 are played with his left hand. The sequence is correct, although the rest part has some errors, the more notes come in simultaneously, the more overtones appear and disturb our detection.

Tone	Note errors	Octave errors	Total notes	Efficiency
Sine	5	0	322	98.44 %
Flute	5	0	322	98.44 %
Oboe	0	4	322	98.75 %
Violin	5	0	322	98.44 %

Table 3.3: *Test results with the generated notes*

3.12 Test of the method

First an artificial sound recording was created with an existing MATLAB program. *Play.m* was developed by Suresh Joel in 2002. It can generate a sequence of notes to a wave file with constant artificial tones. The tone can be sine, flute, oboe, and violin. They have different harmonic numbers, of course it is one in case of sine, five with flute, and six with oboe and violin. Four sequences were generated with all tones from **C2** to **B6** with semitone steps. The test detection was performed with 4096 size original window, zero padded to 16384. The number of the detected notes were 322 for all tones, it means 5 or 6 detections for each note (the generated durations was not equal to the original window size). The efficiency of the detection is shown in Table 3.3. The note errors were in the lower ranges, the place of them was the same in the case of sine, flute and violin. The range of the errors was **C2** to **C3**, and they were related with note changes. In the case of oboe the notes were right, some octave error occurred. The algorithm was tested without octave error checking, and all the detected octaves was wrong. However, there remained 4 errors even with octave error checking. Then notes were played on the bad quality guitar was mentioned in Section 3.10.2. A sequence of notes was played from **E3** to **G#5**. The recorded wave file sounded weird compared with the original, the tone was deformed, but the pitches remained identifiable. The test results had several octave errors both with octave error checking, and without checking. The notes were right, apart from some note change places. The number of the detected notes was 122, there was 101 octave errors and 12 note errors. The reason of the octave errors are the deformed spectrum of the guitar, see Figure 3.8. Without octave errors the efficiency would be approximately 90 %.

3.13 Summary

A fast, efficient, and quite accurate method was introduced for frequency detection in Section 3.5. It can be used for precise measurement or adjustment such as tuning of an instrument.

The further sections were about a note detection method, based on the frequency pairs described in Section 3.6. It can be the base of a polyphonic transcription system with future development.

27

Chapter 4

Chord detection

Chord detection is a kind of polyphonic note detection. Chord detection recognizes the notes sound simultaneously, but it does not care about the number of them, or the right number of the octaves they fall in. For example, both **C3 E4 G3** and **C4 E4 G4** are a C major chord. A chord-matching method will be developed here that can avoid some errors. Chords are very important in popular music, generally they are the bases of songs. It is worthwhile to detect them with their notations and names. They give information about some structural features of a music such as repeated parts, or the played notes in a time interval. A MATLAB function will be developed for chord detection that uses some features of the note detection function introduced in the previous chapter.

4.1 Database of chords

First of all, we have to construct a database, that contains information about different chords. These are patterns that we will use for matching in the detection progress. The examined chord will be represented as a similar pattern. We recall the semitone structure to form patterns that was explained in Chapter 1, it is a practical representation of chords. Here is the database of chords in MATLAB (part of *chord_matching.m*):

```
chordmatrix = [ 1,8,0, 0,0, 0;...      perfect fifth
                1,5,8, 0,0, 0;...
                1,5,8,11,0, 0;...      7
                1,4,8, 0,0, 0;...      m
                1,4,8,11,0, 0;...      m7
                1,5,8,12,0, 0;...      maj7
                1,6,8, 0,0, 0;...      sus4
                1,6,8,11,0, 0;...      7sus4
                1,5,8,10,0, 0;...      6
                1,4,8,10,0, 0;...      m6
                1,5,8,11,3, 0;...      9
```

```
1,4,8,11,3, 0;...      m9
1,5,8,12,3, 0;...      maj9
1,5,8,10,3, 0;...      6/9
1,4,8,10,3, 0;...      m6/9
1,5,8,11,4, 0;...      7(9#)
1,5,8,11,2, 0;...      7(9b)
1,5,9, 0,0, 0;...      +
1,5,9,11,0, 0;...      7(5#)
1,4,7,10,0, 0;...      0
1,5,7, 0,0, 0;...      5b
1,5,7,11,0, 0;...      75b
1,5,8,11,3, 6;...      11
1,5,8,11,3,10];%.      13
```

Each row represents a chord, for example the fourth row represents the minor chord, it has 1-4-8 construction in semitones. 1 is always exists, it represents the root note of the chord. Because of the chords length can be varied, the unused places are padded with zero. These are the most used chords in popular music [5], some of them was introduced in Chapter 1. The first row is the only "chord" with two notes, it was not discussed in Chapter 1. It is a perfect fifth with 1-8 semitone construction. Perfect fifths are played when we do not care for the chord is major or minor but we want to play a base for the song. The prefix 'perfect' indicates, that it sounds good itself, without any additional note. However, every fifth is perfect and sounds good, the reason of this will be explained in Section 4.3. The maximal number of notes in a chord is six, therefore we have six values for each chord with zeros where the chord has less than six notes. The values cover only one octave, although some of the notes in some chords fall into an octave higher by definition. As it was shown in Figure 1.4 and 1.5 on page 6, notes of a chord can repeat themselves in other octaves.

The chord members in *chordmatrix* are considered as sets. Many of these sets are subsets of other sets come some rows later. This will be important in our detection.

4.2   Use of the note detection method in chord detection

The base of the chord detection method is similar to the note detection in Chapter 3. In chord detection needles to care about good time resolution. As it was described in Section 1.4.1, the chord is three or more different notes or pitches sounding simultaneously, *or nearly simultaneously, over a period of time*. Moreover, the duration of a chord can be seconds. Therefore we can use big FFT windows without zero padding. 'Making Love or Expecting Rain' will be the real-world music recording example. The song starts with a church organ part with various chords and fifths. First we apply *note_detect.m* (see the previous chapter) on the first 10 seconds of the song with original window size 32768, zero padded window size 32768 (no padding). Of course nv will be meaningless in this case,

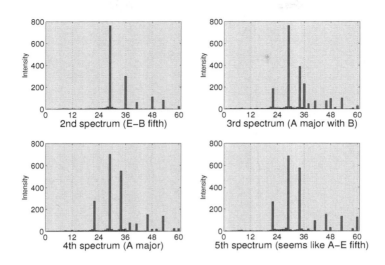

Figure 4.1: *Note spectra in the beginning of the church organ part*

we are curious about the spectra, Figure 4.1 shows the 2nd,3rd,4th,5th element of $ns3d$.

4.3 Connections between overtones and chords

It is worthwhile to examine the connection between overtones and chords. Many of the chords based on perfect fifth, see *chordmatrix* (1-8 in semitones), and major chords has 1-5-8 semitone construction. The explanation of these can be found in overtones. Let's see Table 1.1 again on page 3. We take a note, for example **A3**, that is 220 Hz. The first overtone of **A3** is 440 Hz, it is **A4**. The second overtone has 660 Hz (3·220 Hz), but **A5** is 880 Hz. Is there any note belongs to 660 Hz? Yes, **E5** has almost the same frequency, 659.26 Hz. Therefore the second overtone of **A3** is **E5**. Note **A** and note **E** together is an A-E perfect fifth.

On further examine, the third overtone of **A3** is 880 Hz, it is a note **A** again, **A5**. The fourth overtone is 1100 Hz, the closest note is **C#6** with 1108.73 Hz. Note **A, C#, E** together is the A major chord. Then comes **E** again, **E6** and **G6, A6, B6. G** is the seventh of **A**, therefore **A,C#,E,G** is the A seventh chord. So the followers of **A3** are **A,E,A,C#,E,G,A,B,C**. It is worthwhile to notice, the third and the seventh of the root come much later than the fifth in the overtone sequence.

4.4 Notes and overtones in spectra

First, we focus on the 2nd spectrum in Figure 4.1. The fundamental frequencies are in octave 4, they represent **E4** and **B4**. The overtones of **E4** are **E5,B5,E6,G#6,B6**. And for **B4**, they are **B5,F#6,B6**. Fortunately the spectrum contains only **E** and **B** notes. It is obvious, that note **B** is a separate note. If **B** was an overtone of **E**, the first **B** would appear in place 48. **E** and **B** together is a E-B perfect fifth. A good method could be, if we start examine with the first octaves, looking for peaks. There are no peaks in octave 2 and 3. In octave 4, we can find the two notes. In 5 and 6 the same notes are found.

Now, take a look at the 5th spectrum. There is an improper **B6** in place 60. The question has arisen, it can be an overtone of an other note. **B6** can be an overtone of **E4**, **E5** or **A4**. Both **E5** and **A4** have a peak, but they can be either the first overtones of **E4** and **A3**, or separate notes. However, if **B6** is an overtone, **B5** may has a higher peak. **A,B,E** form together an Esus4 chord, without **B6** it is an A-E perfect fifth.

The 4th spectrum differs only in note **C#5** that has a peak. It is a new note in octave 5, octave 4 has **E4** and **A4** only. **C#5** can not be an overtone (it could be the overtone of **A2**, but **A2** does not have a peak). It is an A major chord. In general the root and the fifth of the root are stressed.

The third spectrum shows a sustained **B** note from the second spectrum. It is not bad, we can recognize it as A major with **B** (with the notation A/B). **B** is a new note in octave 4, but it can not be an overtone. We keep it, although we can't form a chord with it. The detection method will check whether **A,C#,E** is a subset of **A,B,C#,E**. Because it is true, the detected chord will be A major, the auxiliary note will be **B**.

4.5 Estimation of overtones

When we find a new note in an octave, we have to expect that it causes some overtones in later octaves. A notation will be placed in every note that can come into question. It is safer to predict the intensity of overtones, although a notation is enough in most cases. The intensity of overtones is a property of the instrument. A piano tone has different overtones than an oboe or zither tone. Because of this, we use only 0 and 1 notations. The places of the overtones are 12,19,24,28,31,34,36,38 in semitones (according to Table 1.1 and the example in the previous section), where 0 is the root note.

4.6 Peak detection for each octave

As it was seen, the peak detection should be applied for each octave from octave 1. First of all we have to prune the octaves, avoid detection of false peaks. We compute a histogram for the whole spectrum with a lower resolution than the maximal peak of the spectrum:

```
res=10;
```

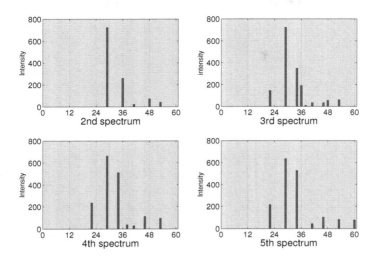

Figure 4.2: *Note spectra after cutting*

```
h=hist(notespectrum,max(notespectrum)/res);
```

The lowest false peaks will be in the beginning of the histogram in a group. The place of the first zero value of the histogram tells the rate of cutting:

```
k=1;
while(h(k) ~= 0) k=k+1; end;

prunedspectrum = notespectrum - res * k;
nc = find(prunedspectrum<0);
prunedspectrum(nc) = 0;
```

The false peaks will disappear, the interesting peaks will be cut a little bit, see Figure 4.1 with Figure 4.2. In case of high disturbing false peaks, some of the weaker notes and overtones can be disappeared after cutting (see note C#5 on the 3rd spectrum, it was almost lost). To avoid this, the resolution of the histogram is scalable, and we can compute the FFT with Hamming or Hanning window because the accuracy of frequencies is indifferent here (the example was computed without any window function). After this, the only thing we have to look for the non-zero places.

4.7 Chord matching

The progress of chord matching begins with initialization of some vectors (part of *chord_matching.m*):

```
chordnotes = zeros(1,12);
prev_chordnotes = zeros(1,12);
overtones = zeros(1,len+37);
blacklisted = [];
```

Vector *chordnotes* is a collector of notes from octaves, *prev_chordnotes* is the previous state of *chordnotes*. For example, **A** was collected from octave 2, and the progress is in octave 3, where **A** and **E** are found. The contents of *chordnotes* are **A** and **E**, while *prev_chordnotes* still contains only **A**. The new notes can be easily determined with the two vectors. When a new note appears, we put 1 to the overtones of the note in vector *overtones*, supposing that *overtones* has zero value in the place of the new note. If *overtones* is 1 in that place, we will not calculate the overtones, the note will be take into vector *blacklisted*, because it can be an overtone of an other note. After the last octave, we have all the notes in *chordnotes* that forms the chord, with suspect and auxiliary notes. Suspect notes are also included in *blacklisted*. We keep them, in case they can participate in forming the chord. The progress of chord matching is very simple (part of *chord_matching.m*):

```
chords = []; auxnotes = [];
for l=24:-1:1                        %24 chords
 for m = 0:11               %12 roots
  ichord = zeros(1,12);
  ichord(mod(chordmatrix(l,1:chordsizes(l))+m-1,12)+1)...
        = 1;
  if length(find(chordnotes-ichord<0)) == 0
   chords = [chords; m+1 l];
   if length(blacklisted) ~=0 chordnotes(blacklisted)=0;
   end;
  end;
 end;
end;
```

All of the chords come into consideration from *chordmatrix* from *bottom to top* (starting with the last chord in *chordmatrix*). It can occur that more than one chord can match with *chordnotes*, because some chords are subset of other ones as it was explained. The result is vector *chords* that contains the detected (matched) chords in order of complexity (the complexity of the chord refers to the row number in *chordmatrix*). For example, the first is Am7, the second is Am/G, the third is A-E perfect fifth/GC, where the notes after '/' are the auxiliary notes. Each of them is taken into consideration, because in some cases more of them can be a satisfying result. The auxiliary notes are calculated from the found chords and from *chordnotes*. If we have any note in *blacklisted*, they will be deleted from *chordnotes* when the first matching occurs. Therefore, we allow only one detected chord that contains any of the suspect notes.

4.8 Selection of good results

There is some consideration in order to select good results.

- If the root notes are equal for all the detected chords, the most complex will be chosen.
  Example: with the 4th spectrum, the contents of *chords* will be A major and A-E perfect fifth with **C#**. Of course, treat **C#** as an auxiliary note has no sense, therefore the most complex chord will be chosen, A major (A).

- If the root notes are not equal, and there was not any suspect note (that can be overtone), any of them can be a good result, considering the rule above, if any of them has pairs with same roots. However, we give preference to the chord which has lower row number in *chordmatrix*.
  Example: with the 3rd spectrum, the contents of *chords* will be Esus4/C# (E sustained with **C#**), A/B, E-B/C#A (E-B perfect fifth with **C#** and **A**), and A-E/C#B. Chords with same roots form groups, the most complex will be selected in each group. Esus4/C# and A/B remain, each of them is a good result, because they are equal with different names. However, A/B will be preferred, because it is easier to recognize. Major and minor chords are well-known chords even for beginners or non-musicians.

- If the root notes are not equal, and there was a suspect note (or more), it can be included in the first result. In this case, if the root of the first result is equal to any of the suspect note, the result will be deleted (the root must be always stressed). If any of the notes are suspected in the first result, the chord will be excepted, and the other results will be investigated according to the rules above. However, the excepted chord can be an alternative result, we should keep it.
  Example: with the 5th spectrum, the contents of *chords* will be Esus4 and A-E. Note **B** is in *blacklisted* and also included in the first chord. Because of **E** is the root note, we keep Esus4 (A-E/B) as an alternative result, the good result will be A-E.

4.9 Detection of chord sequences

MATLAB function *chord_matching.m* was developed for chord detection. The first part of *chord_matching.m* is the database of chords introduced in Section 4.1. The second part collects notes from the pruned octaves, the third is the matching part. They were explained in Section 4.7. The following part is responsible for select the good results, the last part names the chords, using the names of possible notes and chords. The function *chord_detection.m* was developed for detect chord sequences in a song. It uses *note_detection.m* for calculate the note spectra, and then there is an iteration with *chord_matching.m*. The result with the first church organ part is this sequence:

E-B | E-B | A/B | A | A-E | C#m/A | C#m | C#-G# | C#-G# | C#-G#
E-B/C# | E-B | Esus4 | A/B | A-E | C#m/A | C#m | C#-G# | C#-G# | C#-G#

Tone	Number of notes in the chords				
	2	3	4	5	6
Sine	100%	99%	84%	74%	97%
Flute	100%	99%	85%	77%	92%
Oboe	92%	87%	71%	57%	80%
Violin	98%	89%	65%	58%	83%

Table 4.1: *Efficiency of the chord detection algorithm with different tones and chord sizes*

C#m/A I A-E I A6/9 I Bsus4/D# I G#m7 I C#m7 I C#m I E6/9 I F#7sus4/D#
B6/EA I A-E/G# I A-E I A-E I A-E

The similarity of the first two lines comes from the structure of the music, there is a repeated part that almost sounds the same. The chords were tested on a guitar, they cover the notes were played on the organ, sounded the same. However, we got some complex chord, because sometimes the FFT window covers two chords, when chord change occurs. To avoid this, we could use smaller window size. In further work, we can design an algorithm that is looking for these complex chords, and estimates the chord change places (chord change detection).

4.10   Efficiency of the developed chord detection method

The efficiency of the method was tested with the artificial tones described in Section 3.12. The program *chord_test.m* was developed for performing the test, using the tones from Suresh Joels' *play.m*. Separate test was performed for different length chords with all tones. *Chord_test.m* generated a wave file and a text file. The wave files contain 100 random chords with random roots with one of the four tones. The text files contain the names of the generated chords. The file names refer to their content, for example *chord3testflute.wav* and *chord3testflute.txt* are the generated chords with three notes and flute tone. The notes were spread within 3 octaves at random, the length of the chords was 32768 sample points in each case. Then *chord_detection.m* was executed on each wave file. The comparison of the generated and recognized chords has several difficulty, thus it was performed manually. There are many overlaps in the chord names, for example A#m7 and C#6 are exactly the same chords, sometimes the roots are overlapped, for example F#+ and D+ are equivalent. The detection algorithm was forced to show all forms of the detected chords, even the one that contained suspect notes. If any of them was right, the test was successful. The test results are in Table 4.1. As it was expected, the efficiency is lower when there are more overtones with big amplitudes. The structure of the tones are in Table 4.2. The efficiency is also lower with more notes, however there are only two chords with six notes, their results are fairly good.

Tone	Number of harmonic					
	1	2	3	4	5	6
Sine	1	0	0	0	0	0
Flute	1	0.75	0.18	0.18	0.06	0
Oboe	1	1.375	0.75	1	0.45	0.375
Violin	1	0.5	0.43	0.48	0.55	0.76

Table 4.2: *Structure of the test tones, in relative amplitude*

4.11   Summary

A basic chord recognition method was developed in this chapter. It can recognize what kind of notes sound simultaneously, and what type of chord can be constructed with them. Although the pattern matching algorithm is well developed (high-level part), the note detection part needs further development (low-level part). The method works well with one instrument playing, especially if it is lack of bass. For further improvement we should separate the bass and melody frequencies, Goto had a paper about this separation [16].

Chapter 5

Beat detection

This chapter deals with the short explanation of beat. A beat interval detection function will be developed on the basis of DFT and some functions from the previous chapters. Beat detection is a traditional part of musical transcription.

5.1 Beat

When musicians play their instrument, they have to synchronize their play to each other, or to a common tapping. The rhythm of a music is based on this common tapping, that can be a foot tapping, or a beat of a drum. Foot tapping can be helpful for solo musicians, their hands on the instrument will follow the rhythm of the foot tapping. In music analysis, beat is an interval of time, that gives the pulse of the music. The examination of pulses in music can be a good idea, ranges where the sound wave has more intensity than in the other places. On the other hand, beat is a kind of musical meter, see section 2.1.4 on page 13. All kind of meters refer to underlying periodicities of music. Because of this, we should examine some periodic features of the music waveform.

5.2 Periodicity examination with DFT

The periodicities concern on the whole recording, so we have to analyze the whole waveform of the song. The DFT and FFT (introduced in Chapter 3) are able to recognize periodicities, the peaks in the transferred frequency spectrum refer to periodicities in the time domain. Therefore we should apply the DFT on the whole waveform. However, it can be complicated, because of the huge number of sample points. Take our main example of this chapter, 'Every Breath You Take'. The length of the song is 4 minutes and 13 seconds. Consider we use function *wavload.m* (see on page 3.1), then we get a mono wave with 44100 values in every second. The size of the wave will be $(4 \cdot 60 + 13) \cdot 44100 = 11,157,300$ in sample points. MATLAB represents the sample points as a float number between -1 and 1, that takes several bytes. The computation of the DFT would be very slow, we should resample the wave. In practice, it is enough to have one sample per a 1/100 second. With this resolution the

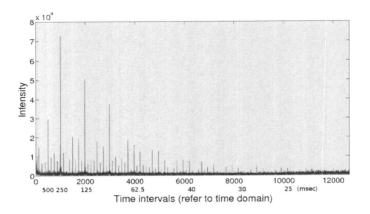

Figure 5.1: *The frequency spectrum of 'Every Breath You Take'*

size of the examined waveform is reduced to 25317 sample points (means 253.17 seconds). The resampling can be computed by the average of the 1/100 second ranges, or by the maximum value of them. Of course it is not possible with the original waveform (the average would be always 0), we have to take the square of it, it will be the energy function of the waveform. Then the result can be taken by a DFT. If we want to use FFT, we have to use zero padding, to enlarge the length to a power of two. However, MATLAB computes only FFT, if the window size is not a power of two, MATLAB computes a certain sequence of FFTs faster than a DFT computation. Therefore we can compute without zero padding with the MATLAB function *fft.m*. The frequency spectrum of 'Every Breath You Take' is shown on Figure 5.1. Each point of the frequency domain represents a time interval of the musical recording, see the second row below the horizontal axis. If L is the length of the frequency spectrum, p is the selected point in the spectrum, the the time interval is $i = L/p$ in the time unit we chose before (that is 1/100 seconds now, the values in the figure are in milliseconds).

There are many peaks that show certain regularities. The highest peak is around 1000, that means $253.17 seconds/1000 = 0.25317 seconds$. The result shows the time interval corresponds to the highest peak. The interval of foot tapping (or rarely the twice of it) is generally between 0.5 and 1 seconds, in this case we have to multiply 0.25317 with 2, the result is 0.50634 seconds. For the precise time interval detection, we recall the method was introduced in Chapter 3, see Equation 3.2 on page 20. Let us assume, that the right value can be found somewhere between 0.5 and 1 seconds (this is exactly an octave in the frequency spectrum). A maximum peak will always be found here, according to several test were applied with various songs and the properties of periodicites (see the tables will be explained later on page 44 and 45). With 'Every Breath You Take', 0.5 seconds correspond to 506 ($253.17second/0.5second = 506.34$) and second 1 is represented on the 253rd point of the DFT transform. The interesting part of the DFT transform can be seen in Figure 5.2.

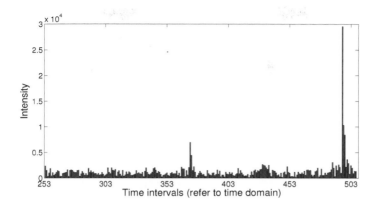

Figure 5.2: *The interesting range of the spectrum (253 -> 1 sec, 506 -> 0.5 sec)*

5.3 Accuracy of the peaks

As it was described in section 3.5, the accuracy of the frequency finder method depends on the frequency we are looking for. For higher frequencies the method gives more accurate results. Similar test methods were executed as in section 3.5 to check the accuracy. There were 100 tests for both lower and higher time intervals. We consider the time intervals between 0.5 and 1 second as lower intervals, and some 1/100 seconds as higher intervals. The length of the random sinusoids were the same as the length of 'Every Breath You Take' in sample points (over 11 million points). Then they were resampled to 25317 points, as it was described above. The results were calculated with Equation 3.2. The left diagram in Figure 5.3 shows the frequencies between 253 and 506 (1 and 0.5 seconds in time intervals). The deviations are too large, 0.0002 seconds mean 9 sample points (with 44100 points in a second). Frequencies between 10000 and 11000 can be detected more accurate, see right diagram. Note, there is a 10^{-8} notation on the horizontal axis, so the values are very little, the accuracy is perfect. The only problem is that we got the interesting peak in the imprecise low range, see Figure 5.2. If we take a closer look at Figure 5.1, the solution will be obvious. The 'fundamental frequency' has 'overtones', and the places of the 'overtones' can be determined.

5.4 Places of the peaks

In 'Every Breath You Take' the drums give mostly the rhythm of the music. The sound of drums has no harmonic structure, they are more similar to a noise, that causes periodical intensity pulsations. However, there are several songs that have no drums at all. Figure 5.4 shows the spectrum of a song, called 'Time of Your Life' that has no drums, just acoustic guitar with singing and strings. This kind of songs have also periodicities, the foot tapping rate can be easily identified. However, the spectrum

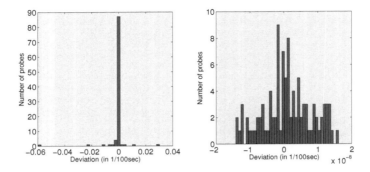

Figure 5.3: *Deviations with two frequency ranges*

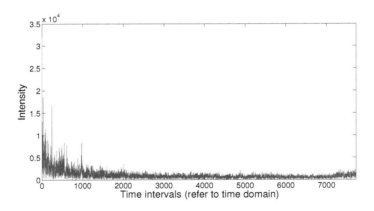

Figure 5.4: *The frequency spectrum of 'Time of Your Life'*

contains less and smaller peaks. There are identifiable peaks at 500, 1000, and 2000 (each of them is double than the previous, octaves). Generally, the distances of the peaks are octaves, and the number of them depends on the song.

5.5 Finding peaks in higher ranges

The peaks in higher ranges might give us more accurate results, than the peak between 0.5 and 1 second. The process of finding the other peaks is very simple. The place of the last found peak is multiplied by two, and the algorithm is looking for an other peak in the neighborhood of the computed double place. If a peak is found near the estimated place, the iteration continues with this peak, it will be the last found. If this peak is far from the estimated, the iteration will be finished. Of course, if we take the following peak in each iteration, the represented time interval will be the half of the previous detected time. Therefore we should correct these values after the iteration with a suitable re-multiplication (multiplication with the proper power of two).

The program *beat_detection.m* was developed to determine these peaks. The input is the song name, the output is the detected peaks, see Table 5.1. The number of detected peaks depends on the song. The values show the detected beats in 1/100 seconds for each peak in each song. We assume that the last value is the most accurate.

5.6 Test of the results

The test was a simple tapping test, the beat was counted in a certain period of time. The results was good mostly, the accuracy of them would be checked by autocorrelation calculations. However, the correlation check was failed, the results were depended of the neighboring ranges were chosen at random from the song. The length of the ranges varied around the minimum and maximum detected beat value. Table 5.3 shows some test results of 'Frontpage of The Sun'. The difference between the maximum and minimum beat values are shown in Table 5.4. They are in sample points, the beat values multiplied by 441 (441 sample points exist in a 1/100 seconds). Take an example, 'I will remember', the minimum detected beat was 609.957 msec, the maximum was 609.993 msec. The difference is 0.036 msec, it is 1.5678 sample points. Because the accuracy test was failed, the measure of accuracy should be this difference. The test of the song 'L'enfant' was difficult, because it does not have stressed rhythm (it is an instrumental song without drums or percussion). The song was opened in a sound file editor program, and the estimated beat was around 0.61 seconds from the waveform. It is interesting, the first half of 'Through The Barricades' has no drums, but the number of the detected peaks are the most, and the deviation is minimal. Theoretically the method can work with songs that have divers rhythm, that means slow and fast parts alternate. In such cases there are two or more peaks in the first range (between 0.5 and 1 seconds). However, this case were not tested, all the songs in the test had constant rhythm. Table 5.2 shows that the results can be different for the

Song Title	peak 1	peak 2	peak 3	peak 4	peak 5	peak 6
'72'	90.3091	90.1941	90.2025	90.2055	90.2040	**90.2042**
'Every Breath You Take'	51.1207	51.1264	51.1294	51.1281	**51.1295**	-
'Frontpage of The Sun'	54.9964	55.0237	55.0237	**55.0156**	-	-
'I Will Remember'	60.9981	60.9993	60.9964	60.9957	**60.9969**	-
'It Hurts'	63.7862	63.8470	63.8429	63.8470	63.8474	**63.8468**
'L'enfant'	61.7353	61.7736	**61.7595**	-	-	-
'Now and Forever'	76.8033	76.8774	76.8705	**76.8589**	-	-
'She's Like The Wind'	96.0517	96.1206	96.0936	96.0796	**96.1187**	-
'Through The Barricades'	82.1230	82.1595	82.1338	82.1273	82.1223	82.1323
'Time of Your Life'	63.5044	63.3089	63.2676	**63.3707**	-	-

Table 5.1: *Time intervals (beats, in 1/100 seconds) were computed from identifiable peaks ('Through The Barricades' has a seventh peak, at 0.821409 seconds)*

MP3 version	54.9964	55.0237	55.0237	**55.0156**
CD version	54.9995	**55.0336**	-	-

Table 5.2: *Results of the two version of 'Frontpage of The Sun'*

same song. The song 'Frontpage of the Sun' was available both on CD and in mp3 format. The beat detections gave different results for the two versions, in spite of the two songs were exactly the same. However, the quality was different, the MP3 files has generally poor high frequency range.

5.7 Summary

This chapter introduced a beat detection algorithm based on DFT. The only result was a time interval, that was the interval of beat or foot tapping. This method is limited for post-process, works only with the full recording of the song. For real-time beat detection, pulse check methods would be efficient.

| Detected results | 54.9964 | 55.0237 | 55.0237 | **55.0156** | |
| Correlation results | 54.9932 | 55.0023 | 55.0091 | 55.0159 | 55.0227 |

Table 5.3: *Some correlation test result of 'Frontpage of The Sun'*

Song Title	Estimated beat in 1/100 seconds	Foot tapping test	Deviation of the results in sample points	Drums in the song
'72'	90.2042	seems good	51	yes
'Every Breath You Take'	51.1295	seems good	4	yes
'Frontpage of The Sun'	55.0156	seems good	12	yes
'I Will Remember'	60.9969	seems good	2	yes
'It Hurts'	63.8468	seems good	27	yes
'L'enfant'	61.7595	ambiguous	17	no
'Now and Forever'	76.8589	seems good	33	no
'She's Like The Wind'	96.1187	seems good	30	partly
'Through The Barricades'	82.1409	seems good	16	partly
'Time of Your Life'	63.3707	seems good	104	no

Table 5.4: *Foot tapping test of the estimated results*

Chapter 6

Summary of the thesis

Musical transcription includes several components, some of them were introduced in this thesis. A full transcription system has to be capable of recognizing every feature of music that can affect the behavior of sounded notes. Notes have certain pitches and durations, they also have overtones. Notes can form chords, chords can form higher structures with the help of beat and lyrics. Beat is the base of note durations, while chords can be the base of note pitches. The pitches and durations have higher level structures in music, that means not all combinations of notes sound good. Notes can be sounded by more than one sources, instruments in general. It makes harder the detection of individual notes, the transcription system has to have the capability of estimation some features of notes that was not examined in this thesis. The existing literature prefers low-level digital signal processing techniques to examine and estimate as many features as possible.

In contrast with that, we rather take the musical aspects of basic transcription techniques. The chord detection method in Chapter 4 was designed to recognize patterns that have high-level musical meaning, the note detection part of it was inherited from the basic note detection method introduced in Chapter 3. The accurate frequency detection method was designed to detect any kind of pitches, and it was useful in beat detection introduced in Chapter 5. The introduced beat detection method can determine certain important time intervals, they are parts of the music structure.

The developed tools can be the basis of a future musical information system.

APPENDIX

List of the developed MATLAB programs

Note detection

• generate_notes.m

computes frequencies of notes

Function definition : **notes = generate_notes(bottom, top)**

Inputs : the lowest (*bottom*) and the highest (*top*) note in semitones, where **C2** = 0

Output : sequence of frequencies (*notes*), see Table 1.1

Source code:

```
function notes=generate_notes(bottom,top);

bottom=1;              %  1 ~ C2
top=60;                % 60 ~ B6

notes = [];

next_note_m = 2^(1/12);

%%% Note A4 is 440 Hz
note_a = 440;

sh = note_a;

%%% Computing the notes above 440 Hz
for k = 34:top
    notes(k) = sh;
    sh = sh * next_note_m;
end

sh = note_a;
```

```
%%% Computing the notes below 440 Hz
for k = 33:-1:bottom
    sh = sh / next_note_m;
    notes(k) = sh;
end
```

- **translate_notes.m**

  maps the frequencies according to a certain FFT window size

  Function definition : **mapped_notes = translate_notes(notes, window)**

  Inputs : *notes* is the frequency sequence generated by *generate_notes.m*
  window is the size of the FFT window

  Output : sequence of mapped frequencies (*mapped_notes*)

  Source code:

  ```
  function mapped_notes=translate_notes(notes,window)

  window = 16384;
  wt = window/44100;

  wscale = wt*notes;

  mapped_notes = [];

  for k = 1:length(wscale)
      mapped_notes = [mapped_notes;
       fix(wscale(k)) fix(wscale(k))+1];
  end

  mapped_notes = mapped_notes';
  ```

- **frequency_index.m**

  chooses the interesting frequencies from a spectrum according to the frequencies of notes

  Function definition : **notes_intensity=frequency_index(s,mapped_notes)**

  Inputs : *s* is the FFT spectrum
  mapped_notes is the mapped frequency sequence generated by *translate_notes.m*

Output : sequence of note intensities in the FFT window (*notes_intensity*, called 'note spectrum')

Source code:

```
function notes_intensity=frequency_index(s,mapped_notes)

t = [];

for k=1:length(mapped_notes(1,:))
    t = [t s(mapped_notes(1,k))+s(mapped_notes(2,k))];
end
```

- **note_detection.m**

  detects notes in a monophonic music wave file

  Function definition :

  function [ns3d nv nd3d] = note_detection(filename,origw,window, notedet)

  Inputs : *filename* is the name of the song FFT

  origw is the original window size

  window is the zero-padded window size

  notedet is 1 for note detection, 0 outputs only note frequencies

  Outputs : *ns3d* is the sequence of note spectra (the vectors same as *notes_intensity* vector in *frequency_index.m*)

  nv is the sequence of note names (with octave notation); empty when *notedet* is 0

  nd3d is the same as *ns3d*, but the vectors contains only the intensity of the detected note; empty when *notedet* is 0

  Source code:

```
function [ns3d nv nd3d] = note_detection(filename,origw,
window,notedet);

%notedet = 1;          %%%% 1 allow note detection,
                       %%%% 0 only ns3d will be computed

%%%%%%%%%%%%%%%%%%%%%%%%%%% generate_notes.m %%%%%

bottom=1;             %  1 ~ C2
top=60;               %  60 ~ B6
```

```
notes = [];

next_note_m = 2^(1/12);

%%% Note A4 is 440 Hz
note_a = 440;

sh = note_a;

%%% Computing the notes above 440 Hz
for k = 34:top
    notes(k) = sh;
    sh = sh * next_note_m;
end

sh = note_a;

%%% Computing the notes below 440 Hz
for k = 33:-1:bottom
    sh = sh / next_note_m;
    notes(k) = sh;
end

%%%%%%%%%%%%%%%%%%%%%%%%%%%%%% translate_notes.m %%%%%%

%window = 16384;
wt = window/44100;

wscale = wt*notes;

mapped_notes = [];

for k = 1:length(wscale)
    mapped_notes = [mapped_notes;
     fix(wscale(k)) fix(wscale(k))+1];
end

mapped_notes = mapped_notes';
```

```
%%%%%%%%%%%%%%%%%%%%%%%%%%%%%%%%%%%%%%%%%%%%%%%%%%%%%%

note_names ={
'C2','C#2','D2','D#2','E2','F2','F#2','G2','G#2','A2',
'A#2','B2',
'C3','C#3','D3','D#3','E3','F3','F#3','G3','G#3','A3',
'A#3','B3',
'C4','C#4','D4','D#4','E4','F4','F#4','G4','G#4','A4',
'A#4','B4',
'C5','C#5','D5','D#5','E5','F5','F#5','G5','G#5','A5',
'A#5','B5',
'C6','C#6','D6','D#6','E6','F6','F#6','G6','G#6','A6',
'A#6','B6'};

%%%%%%%%%%%%%%%%%%%%%%%%%%%%%%%%%%%

y = wavread(filename);

nv = []; ns3d=[]; nd3d=[];
cn = fix(length(y)/origw);

for k = 1:cn

    s = abs(fft( [y( ((k-1)*origw + 1):k*origw )'
    zeros(1,window-origw)] ));
    s(1) = [];
    %bar(s(1:400));

    %%%%%%%%%%%%%%%%% frequency_index.m %%%%%%%%%%%%%%%%%%%

    t = [];
    for l=1:length(mapped_notes(1,:))
        t = [t s(mapped_notes(1,l))+s(mapped_notes(2,l))];
    end

    %%%%%%%%%%%%%%%%%%%%%%%%%%%%%%%%%%%%%%%%%%%%%%%%%%%%%%%

    %t(1:36) = 0;
```

```
%t=prune_spectrum(t);
ns3d=[ns3d; t];
if notedet
    [mi mp] = max(t);


        %octave error checking
        [mi mpl] = max(t(1:mp-1));
        if mpl == mp-12 mp = mpl; end;   %correction


        nv = [nv note_names(mp)];
        dt = zeros(1,length(t));  dt(mp)=1;
        nd3d=[nd3d; dt];
    end;
end;
```

• **find_freq.m**

Finds the accurate frequency of the largest peak in a FFT spectrum

Function definition :

freq=find_freq(notespectrum,res)

Inputs : *notespectrum* is the spectrum

    res is frequency resolution of the spectrum

Output : *freq* is the accurate frequency of the highest peak

Source code:

```
function freq=find_freq(notespectrum,res);

[ym1 xm1] = max(notespectrum);          %the largest peak
notespectrum(xm1) = 0;
[ym2 xm2] = max(xm1-1:xm1+1));          %largest neighbour

if xm2 == 3 freq = (xm1 + (ym2 / (ym1 + ym2)) ) * res;
end; %right or
if xm2 == 1 dreq = (xm1 - 1 + (ym1 / (ym1 + ym2)) ) * res;
end; %left
```

53

• **deviation.m**

Deviation test program for find_freq.m

Function definition : **deviation**

Source code:

```
r=44100/8192;
s=pi*2/44100;
x=1:44100;
fe=[]; fv=[]; dfv=[];

minfreq=20;
maxfreq=2000;

for l=1:100

        f=rand*(maxfreq-minfreq)+minfreq;
        y=sin(s*f*x+rand*pi);

        t=abs(fft(y(1:8192)));

        %t=abs(fft([y(1:4096) zeros(1,4096+8192+16384)]));
        %t=abs(fft(y(1:8192).*hamming(8192)'));
        %t=abs(fft(y(1:8192).*hanning(8192)'));

        t=t(2:4000);

        [ym1 xm1] = max(t);
        t(xm1) = 0;
        [ym2 xm2] = max(t);

        if (xm2-xm1) == 1 df = (xm1+(ym2/(ym1+ym2))) * r; end;
        if (xm1-xm2) == 1 df = (xm2+(ym1/(ym1+ym2))) * r; end;

        fv = [fv f];
        dfv= [dfv df];

    end

    fe=fv-dfv;
```

Chord detection

- ## prune_spectrum.m

    cuts the false little peaks in a note spectrum

    Function definition : **prunedspectrum = prune_spectrum (notespectrum)**

    Input : *notespectrum* is the note spectrum

    Output : *prunedspectrum* is the spectrum without false peaks

    Source code:

    ```
    function prunedspectrum = prune_spectrum (notespectrum)

    res=10;

    h=hist(notespectrum,max(notespectrum)/res);

    k=1;
    while(h(k) ~= 0) k=k+1; end;

    prunedspectrum = notespectrum - res * k;
    nc = find(prunedspectrum<0);
    prunedspectrum(nc) = 0;
    ```

- ## chord_naming.m

    gives a name for a root note and chord type, including the auxiliary notes

    Function definition : **chordname=chord_naming(chord,auxnotes)**

    Inputs : *chord* is a vector, a root note and a chord type (1-24)

            auxnotes is the sequence of auxiliary notes

    Output : *chordname* is the name of the chord

    Source code:

    ```
    function chordname=chord_naming(chord,auxnotes)

    notes =  {'C','C#','D','D#','E','F',
    'F#','G','G#','A','A#','B'};
    fifths = {'G','G#','A','A#','B','C',
    ```

```
'C#','D','D#','E','F' ,'F#'};

chordnames  = {'fifth','','7','m','m7','maj7','sus4',
'7sus4','6','m6','9','m9','maj9','6/9','m6/9','7(9#)',
'7(9b)','+','7(5#)','0','5b','75b','11','13'};

chordname = [];

if chord(2) == 1
    chordname=strcat(notes(chord(1)),'-',fifths(chord(1)));
else
    chordname=strcat(notes(chord(1)),chordnames(chord(2)));
end;

if length(find(auxnotes==0)) ~= 12

    chordname = strcat(chordname,'/');
    for k=1:12
      if auxnotes(k) chordname=strcat(chordname,notes(k));
    end;
end;
```

• chord_matching.m

Determines the chord name of a note spectrum

Function definition :

**chordname=chord_matching(notespectrum,show_otherforms,
show_alternatives)**

Inputs : *notespectrum* is the note spectrum

when *show_otherforms* is 1, all the forms of the chord will be detected

when *show_alternatives* is 1, the alternative chord will be also detected

Output : *chordname* is the name(s) of the detected chord

Source code:

```
function chordname=chord_matching(notespectrum,
show_otherforms,show_alternatives)

%%% database of chords
```

```
chordmatrix = [ 1,8,0, 0,0, 0;...      perfect fifth
                1,5,8, 0,0, 0;...
                1,5,8,11,0, 0;...      7
                1,4,8, 0,0, 0;...      m
                1,4,8,11,0, 0;...      m7
                1,5,8,12,0, 0;...      maj7
                1,6,8, 0,0, 0;...      sus4
                1,6,8,11,0, 0;...      7sus4
                1,5,8,10,0, 0;...      6
                1,4,8,10,0, 0;...      m6
                1,5,8,11,3, 0;...      9
                1,4,8,11,3, 0;...      m9
                1,5,8,12,3, 0;...      maj9
                1,5,8,10,3, 0;...      6/9
                1,4,8,10,3, 0;...      m6/9
                1,5,8,11,4, 0;...      7(9#)
                1,5,8,11,2, 0;...      7(9b)
                1,5,9, 0,0, 0;...      +
                1,5,9,11,0, 0;...      7(5#)
                1,4,7,10,0, 0;...      0
                1,5,7, 0,0, 0;...      5b
                1,5,7,11,0, 0;...      75b
                1,5,8,11,3, 6;...      11
                1,5,8,11,3,10];        %13


chordsizes = [2,3,4,3,4,4,3,4,4,4,
5,5,5,5,5,5,5,3,4,4,3,4,6,6];

%%% prepare overtone estimation

overtone_places=[0,12,19,24,28,31,34,36,37];
maxovertones=6;

%%% prepare note collection

len=length(notespectrum);

chordnotes = zeros(1,12);                %actual collected
%chord notes
```

```
prev_chordnotes = zeros(1,12);          %previous of this
overtones = zeros(1,len+37);
blacklisted = [];

ko=0;

%%%%%%%%%%%%% note collection part %%%%%%%%%%%%%%%%

for k=1:5

        sel_notes = notespectrum(ko+1:ko+12);

    %octavenotes=(sign(notespectrum(ko+1:ko+12)));
    octavenotes=(sign(sel_notes));

    chordnotes=chordnotes | octavenotes;

    newnotes=find(prev_chordnotes-chordnotes<0);

    if length (newnotes)

     for l=1:length(newnotes)

            if overtones(ko+newnotes(l)) == 0

                for m=1:maxovertones
                overtones(ko+newnotes(l)+overtone_places(m))=1;
                end;

      else
                blacklisted=[blacklisted newnotes(l)];
            end;

       end;

    end;

    ko = ko + 12;
    prev_chordnotes=chordnotes;
```

```
end;

%%%%% Chord matching part %%%%%%%%%%

chords = []; auxnotes = [];

for l=24:-1:1                %24 chords

        for m = 0:11        %12 roots

            ichord = zeros(1,12);
            ichord(  mod(chordmatrix(l,1:chordsizes(l))+
    m-1,12)+1  ) = 1;

            if length(find(chordnotes-ichord<0)) == 0
                chords = [chords; m+1 l];
                if length(blacklisted) ~=0
chordnotes(blacklisted)=0;
end;
    end;
        end;
end;

%%%%% Auxiliary notes part %%%%%%

nch = size(chords);
auxnotes = zeros(nch(1),12);

for k = 1:nch(1)

    root=chords(k,1);
    chord=chords(k,2);

    auxnotes(k,:)= chordnotes;
    auxnotes(k,mod((chordmatrix(
     chord ,1:chordsizes(chord))+root-1)-1,12)+1)= 0;

end
```

```
% chords
% auxnotes

%%%%% Chord selecting part %%%%%%%%%%

alter_chord = [];

if length(blacklisted) ~= 0

    poss_over=zeros(1,12);
    poss_over(blacklisted)=1;
    poss_chord=zeros(1,12);
    poss_chord(mod((chordmatrix(
      chords(1,2) ,1:chordsizes(chords(1,2)))+
chords(1,1)-1)-1,12)+1)=1;

    if length(find(poss_chord-poss_over<0)) == 0

        if length(find(blacklisted==chords(1,1))) == 0
            alter_chord = chords(1,:);
            alter_aux = auxnotes(1,:);
        end;

        chords(1,:) = [];
        auxnotes(1,:) = [];
    end;
end;

cs = size(chords); cs(2) = [];

if cs == 0 & alter_chord
chordname = chord_naming(alter_chord,alter_aux); return;
end

if cs > 1                       %check whether has groups

    k = 2;
    r = chords(k-1,1);
```

```matlab
    while (r ~= chords(k,1) & k < cs)
      r = chords(k,1);
k=k+1;
    end;

    if k <=cs
        chords(k:end,:) = [];
        auxnotes(k:end,:) = [];
    end;

end;

cs = size(chords); cs(2) = [];

if cs > 1                         %cut less complex, if grouped

    rs = chords(:,1)';
    rr = find(rs==rs(1));
    if length(rr) > 1
        chords(rr(2):end,:)=[];
        auxnotes(rr(2):end,:)=[];
    end;

end
%
% chords
% auxnotes

%%%%%%%%% Chord naming part %%%%%%

%show_otherforms = 1;
%show_alternatives = 1;

cs = size(chords); cs(2) = [];

if cs == 0 chordname = {'???'};
else

    chordname = chord_naming(chords(cs,:),auxnotes(cs,:));
```

```
end


if cs > 1 & show_otherforms
    chordname = strcat(chordname,' ( ');
    cs = cs - 1;
    while (cs >= 1)
    chordname = strcat(chordname,
     chord_naming(chords(cs,:),auxnotes(cs,:)), ' ');
    cs=cs-1;
    end;
    chordname = strcat(chordname,')');
end


if length(alter_chord) ~= 0 & show_alternatives

    chordname = strcat(chordname,
     ' (can be:',chord_naming(alter_chord,alter_aux),' )');
end;
```

• chord_detection.m

Detects the chords in a wave file

Function definition :

chords=chord_detection(filename,window,
show_otherforms, show_alternatives)

Inputs : $filename$ is the name of the wave file

$window$ is the size of the FFT windows

when $show\_otherforms$ is 1, all the forms of the chord will be detected

when $show\_alternatives$ is 1, the alternative chord will be also detected

Output : $chords$ is the sequence of chordnames in the required form

Source code:

```
function chordseq = chord_detection(filename, window,
show_otherforms, show_alternatives);

spectra = note_detection(filename,window,window,0);
spectras = size(spectra);
```

```
chordseq = [];

for k=1:spectras(1)

    spectrum = spectra(k,:);
    spectrum = prune_spectrum(spectrum);

        max_sp = max(spectrum);
        spectrum = spectrum-max_sp*0.2;
        neg_pl = find(spectrum<0);
        spectrum (neg_pl) = 0;


    %figure(k);
    %bar(spectrum)

    chordseq=[chordseq,
      chord_matching(spectrum,
        show_otherforms, show_alternatives)];

end;
```

• chord_test.m

Makes test wave files for chord_detection, using the tones of play.m

Function definition : **chord_test**

Inputs : there are several scalable variables within the program that affects the properties of the generated chords

Outputs : two files, a wave file and a text file with the generated chords

Source code:

```
function chord_test

chordmatrix = [ 1,8,0, 0,0, 0;...      perfect fifth

                1,5,8, 0,0, 0;...
                1,4,8, 0,0, 0;...      m
                1,6,8, 0,0, 0;...      sus4
                1,5,9, 0,0, 0;...      +
```

63

```
                    1,5,7, 0,0, 0;...      5b

                    1,5,8,11,0, 0;...      7
                    1,4,8,11,0, 0;...      m7
                    1,5,8,12,0, 0;...      maj7
                    1,6,8,11,0, 0;...      7sus4
                    1,5,8,10,0, 0;...      6
                    1,4,8,10,0, 0;...      m6
                    1,5,9,11,0, 0;...      7(5#)
                    1,4,7,10,0, 0;...      0
                    1,5,7,11,0, 0;...      75b

                    1,5,8,11,3, 0;...      9
                    1,4,8,11,3, 0;...      m9
                    1,5,8,12,3, 0;...      maj9
                    1,5,8,10,3, 0;...      6/9
                    1,4,8,10,3, 0;...      m6/9 ·
                    1,5,8,11,4, 0;...      7(9#)
                    1,5,8,11,2, 0;...      7(9b)

                    1,5,8,11,3, 6;...      11
                    1,5,8,11,3,10];%       13


chordsizes = [0,1,6,15,22,24];

chordtranslate = [1, 2,4,7,18,21,
3,5,6,8,9,10,19,20,22,
11,12,13,14,15,16,17,23,24];


%%%%%%% generate_notes.m %%%%%%%%%%%%%%%%%%%%%%%%%

bottom=1;              %  1 ~ C2
top=60;                % 60 ~ B6

notes = [];

next_note_m = 2^(1/12);
```

```
%%% Note A4 is 440 Hz
note_a = 440;

sh = note_a;

%%% Computing the notes above 440 Hz
for k = 34:top
    notes(k) = sh;
    sh = sh * next_note_m;
end

sh = note_a;

%%% Computing the notes below 440 Hz
for k = 33:-1:bottom
    sh = sh / next_note_m;
    notes(k) = sh;
end

chordlengths = 32768;
chordsizemin = 6;
chordsizemax = 6;
chordnumbers = 100;
instrument = 'violin';
testsongname = 'chord6testviolin';

fid = fopen(strcat(testsongname,'.txt'),'w');

testsong = [];
w = 1/44100;
t = 1:chordlengths;

chordsizediff = chordsizes (chordsizemax) -
chordsizes (chordsizemin-1);
chordsizebegin = chordsizes (chordsizemin - 1) + 1;

for k = 1:chordnumbers
```

```
rootnote = fix (rand * 48);
chordnum = fix (rand * chordsizediff + chordsizebegin);
chord = chordmatrix (chordnum,:);

chordname =
 chord_naming ([mod(rootnote,12)+1,
   chordtranslate(chordnum)],zeros(1,12));
fprintf(fid,'%s\n',char(chordname));

notenumbers = find(chord==0);
if length(notenumbers) == 0 notenumbers = 6;
else
    notenumbers = notenumbers (1) - 1;
end

actualchord = zeros(1,chordlengths);

for l = 1:notenumbers

    actnote=rootnote+chord(l)+round(rand*2-1)*12;
    if actnote > 60 actnote = actnote-12; end;
    if actnote < 1 actnote = actnote+12; end;

    w = 1/44100 * notes(actnote);

    switch(instrument)

case 'sine'

x1=sin((2*pi*w).*t);

case 'flute'

x1=sin((2*pi*w).*t)+ 0.75*sin((2*pi*w*2).*t) +
 0.18*sin((2*pi*w*3).*t) + 0.18*sin((2*pi*w*4).*t) +
 0.06*sin((2*pi*w*5).*t);

case 'oboe'
```

```
x1=sin((2*pi*w).*t)+ 1.375*sin((2*pi*w*2).*t) +
 0.75*sin((2*pi*w*3).*t) + sin((2*pi*w*4).*t) +
 0.45*sin((2*pi*w*5).*t) + 0.375*sin((2*pi*w*6).*t);

case 'violin'

x1=sin((2*pi*w).*t)+ 0.5*sin((2*pi*w*2).*t) +
 0.43*sin((2*pi*w*3).*t) + 0.48*sin((2*pi*w*4).*t) +
 0.55*sin((2*pi*w*5).*t) + 0.76*sin((2*pi*w*6).*t);

    end

actualchord = actualchord+x1;

 end;

 testsong = [testsong actualchord/notenumbers];
end;

wavwrite (testsong,44100,16,testsongname);
fclose (fid);
```

Beat detection

- ## deviation_beat.m

  Deviation test program for peaks in different ranges

  Function definition : **deviation_beat**

  Source code:

```
r = 100;
res = fix(44100 / r);

len = 11165231;
lenex = fix(len / res);

s=pi*2/len;
x=1:len;
fe=[]; fv=[]; dfv=[];
```

```
te=[]; tv=[]; dtv=[];

for l=1:100

    f=rand*1000+10020;
    ti = len / f;

    y=sin(s*f*x+rand*pi);

    m = 0;
    ys = [];

        while m < len - res
         ys = [ys sum(y(m+1:m+res))];
         m = m + res;
        end

    length(ys)

    t=abs(fft(ys));
    %t=abs(fft([y(1:4096) zeros(1,4096+8192+16384)]));
    %t=abs(fft(y(1:8192).*hamming(8192)'));
    %t=abs(fft(y(1:8192).*hanning(8192)'));

    lenex=length(t);

    t=t(2:lenex/2);

    [ym1 xm1] = max(t);
    t(xm1) = 0;
    [ym2 xm2] = max(t);

    if (xm2-xm1) == 1 df = (xm1+(ym2/(ym1+ym2))); end;
    if (xm1-xm2) == 1 df = (xm2+(ym1/(ym1+ym2))); end;

    fv = [fv f];
    dfv= [dfv df];
    %fe = [fe f - df];
    tv = [tv ti / res];
```

```
        dtv= [dtv lenex/df];

end

fe=fv-dfv;
te=tv-dtv;
```

• beat_detection.m

Detects the beat in a wave file that contains a constant rhythm song

Function definition : **beat510 = beat_detection(name)**

Input : *name* is the name of the wave file

Output : *beat510* is the estimated beats between 0.5 and 1 seconds, in 1/100 seconds

Source code:

```
function beat510 = beat_detection(name)

rest = 1 / 100;
res = 44100 * rest;

%%%%%%%%% Load song %%%%%%%%%%

fprintf ('Load song');
a = wavload (name,0);

fprintf ('\nCut leading zeros');

x=1;

while a(x) == 0 x=x+1; end

fprintf ('\ncut %i zeros (%i unit)',x-1,round((x-1)/res));
a = a(x:end);

fprintf ('\nPadding zeros in the end');
a = [a zeros(1,res-mod (length(a),res) )];

%%%%%%%%% Computing energy function %%%%%%%%%%%%%
```

```
e = a .^ 2;

%%%%%%%%% Downsampling %%%%%%

x = 0; em = [];

fprintf ('\nDownsampling');
while x < length (a)
    em = [em sum(e(x+1:x+res))];
     %it could be max instead of sum
    x = x + res;
end

fprintf ('\nComputig FFT');
l = length(em);
s = abs(fft(em)); s(1) = [];
%we don't need the constant member
ws = 5;

fprintf ('\nExploring peaks');

%************************************************************
%
% We compute the first peak between 0.5 and 1 second
%
%************************************************************

window = fix(l*rest):fix(l*rest*2);
%window between 0.5 and 1
offset = fix(l*rest) - 1;

[ym1 xm1] = max(s(window));    %calculate the peak position
s(offset + xm1) = 0;
[ym2 xm2] = max(s(offset+xm1-1:offset+xm1+1));

if xm2 == 3 df=(offset+xm1+(ym2/(ym1+ym2)));
end;
if xm2 == 1 df=(offset+xm1-1+(ym1/(ym1 + ym2)));
end;
```

```
beat = 1 / df;                          %the first estimated beat
ef = df;


%*******************************************************
%
% Then come the multiples of the first peak
%
%*******************************************************

while ef < 1 / 2

    ef = round(ef * 2);
    window = ef-ws:ef+ws;
    offset = ef-ws-1;

    [ym1 xm1] = max(s(window));

    abs(xm1-ws)
     %difference between predicted and found peak
    if abs(xm1-ws) > 2 break; end;
     %quit when this difference is big


    s(offset + xm1) = 0;
    [ym2 xm2] = max(s(offset+xm1-1:offset+xm1+1));


    if xm2 == 3 df=(offset+xm1+(ym2/(ym1 + ym2)));
    end;
    if xm2 == 1 df=(offset+xm1-1+(ym1/(ym1 + ym2)));
    end;

    beat (end+1) = 1 / df;
    ef = df;

end;


beat510 = beat;
```

```
for x = length(beat):-1:2

    beat510(x) = beat510(x) * 2 ^ (x-1);      %correction

end;
```

- **beat_test.m**

  Correlation test of the detected beat values

  Function definition : **cc = beat_test(song,beat)**

  Inputs : *song* is the name of the wave file
  beat is the detected beats, same as *beat510* in *beat_detection.m*

  Output : *cc* is the estimated beats with autocorrelation tests

  Source code:

```
function cc=beat_test(song, beat)

a = wavload(song,0);
len = round(length(a)/44100);

cc = [];

for nop = 1:10

    start=round(44100*rand*(len-1));

    lb = round(min(beat*441));
    hb = round(max(beat*441));

    sb = round(lb-(hb-lb)/2);
    eb = round(hb+(hb-lb)/2);

    corr = [];

    for ab = sb:eb

        b = corrcoef(a(start:start+ab),
         a(start+ab+1:start+ab+1+ab));
        c = b(1,2);
```

```
    corr = [corr c];

end;

[yl xl] = min(corr);
[yh xh] = max(corr);

lc = (sb+xl-1)/441;
hc = (sb+xh-1)/441;

fprintf ('\nmin:%f',lc);
fprintf ('\nmax:%f\n',hc);

figure (nop);
plot(corr);

%if length(find(cc==lc)) == 0 cc = [cc lc]; end;
if length(find(cc==hc)) == 0 cc = [cc hc]; end;

end;
```

Other programs

• play.m

Author : **Suresh Joel**

Makes wave files of notes from a basic 'score' text file

Function definition : **play(infile,instrument,outfile)**

Input : *infile* is the 'score' file including note frequencies and durations

instrument is the type of the generated tone, can be 'sine', 'flute', 'oboe', or 'violin'

Output : *outfile* is the generated wave file

• wavload.m

Load and converts a stereo wave file into a mono wave

Function definition : **y = wavload(f,size)**

Inputs : *f* is the name of the stereo wave file

size is the samples to be read

73

Output : y is the mono wave vector normalized between -1 and 1

Source code:

```
function y = wavload(f,size)

fn = length ( f(:,1) );

minlength=44100*11;

y = zeros (fn,minlength);

for x=1:fn,

    [signal fq nbits] = wavread ( f(x,:) );

    len = length(signal);
    if len<minlength, minlength=len; end

    signal (:,1) = ( signal (:,1) + signal (:,2) ) / 2;
    signal (:,2) = [];

    y (x,1:len) = signal';

end

if size ~= 0, minlength = size; end

y (:,minlength+1:44100*11) = [];
```

List of songs

- **72**

  Appears in Chapter 5.

  Music and Lyrics by **Per Gessle**

  Performed by **Gyllene Tider**

  Released on **Finn Fem Fel** album (2004)

- **Den Tunna Linjen**

  Appears in Section 3.11.

  Music and Lyrics by **Per Gessle**

  Performed by **Per Gessle** and **Marie Fredriksson**

  Released on Per Gessle's second solo album, **Scener** (1985)

- **Every Breath You Take**

  Appears in Chapter 5.

  Music and Lyrics by **The Police**

  Performed by **The Police**

  Released on **Synchronicity** album (1983)

- **Frontpage of The Sun**

  Appears in Chapter 5.

  Music by **Kai Wingenfelder, Christof Stein-Schneider, Gero Drnek**

  Lyrics by **Kai Wingenfelder**

  Performed by **Fury in the Slaughterhouse**

  Released on **Nowhere Fast** album (1998)

- **Good Riddance (Time of Your Life)**

Appears in Chapter 5.

Music and Lyrics by **Green Day**

Performed by **Green Day**

Released on **Nimrod** album (1997)

- ## I Will Remember

  Appears in Chapter 5.

  Music and Lyrics by **Steve Lukather** and **Stan Lynch**

  Performed by **Toto**

  Released on **Tambu** album (1995)

- ## It Hurts

  Appears in Chapter 5.

  Music and Lyrics by **Per Gessle**

  Performed by **Roxette**

  Released on **The Ballad Hits** album (2002)

- ## L'enfant

  Appears in Chapter 5.

  Music by **Vangelis**

  Performed by **Vangelis**

  Released on **Opéra Sauvage** album (1979)

- **Making Love or Expecting Rain**

  Appears in Chapter 4.

  Music and Lyrics by **Per Gessle**

  Performed by **Per Gessle, Helena Josefsson, Clarence Öfwerman, Christoffer Lundquist** and **Jens Janson**

  Released on Per Gessle's fifth solo album, **Son of a Plumber** (2005)

- **Now and Forever**

  Appears in Chapter 5.

  Music and Lyrics by **Richard Marx**

  Performed by **Richard Marx**

  Released on **Paid Vacation** album (1994)

- **She's Like The Wind**

  Appears in Chapter 5.

  Music and Lyrics by **Patrick Swayze** and **Stacy Widelitz**

  Performed by **Patrick Swayze** and **Wendy Fraser**

  Released on **Dirty Dancing Original Soundtrack** album (1987)

- **Things Like This**

  Appears in Chapter 3.

  Music by **Christof Stein-Schneider, Gero Drnek, Christian Decker, Rainer Schuman, Thorsten Wingenfelder, Kai Wingenfelder**

  Lyrics by **Kai Wingenfelder, Christof Stein-Schneider**

  Performed by **Fury in the Slaughterhouse**

  Released on **The Color Fury** album (2002)

- ## Through The Barricades

  Appears in Chapter 5.

  Music and Lyrics by **Spandau Ballet**

  Performed by **Spandau Ballet**

  Released on **Through The Barricades** album (1986)

- ## Wish You Were Here

  Appears in Section 1.4.8.

  Music and Lyrics by **Roger Waters** and **David Gilmour**

  Performed by **Pink Floyd**

  Released on **Wish You Were Here** album (1975)

Bibliography

[1] Guitaretab! *http://www.guitaretab.com.*

[2] Mathworld. *http://www.mathworld.com.*

[3] Wikipedia: The free encyclopedia. *http://www.wikipedia.org.*

[4] Samer A. Abdallah and Mark D. Plumbley. *Polyphonic Music Transcription by Non-Negative Sparse Coding of Power Spectra.* University of London.

[5] Remo Andrásik. *Gitár kézikönyv - elméleti és gyakorlati alapismeretek I-II. (hungarian).* Instrument Reklám Bt., Budapest, Hungary.

[6] I. Barbancho, A. M. Barbancho, A. Juardo, and L.J. Tardón. *Transcription of piano recordings.* Universidad de Málaga, Málaga, Spain, 2004.

[7] Juan P. Bello, Giuliano Monti, and Mark Sandler. *Techniques for Automatic Music Transcription.* King's College London.

[8] C. Chafe, D. Jaffe, K. Kashima, B. Mont-Reynaud, and J. Smith. Techniques for note identification in polyphonic music. *International Computer Music Conference 6(1): 399-405*, 1985.

[9] C. Chafe, B. Mont-Reynaud, and L. Rush. Towards an intelligent editor of digital audio: recognition of musical constructs. *Computer Music Journal. 6(1):30-41*, 1982.

[10] Jonathan J. A. Darch. *An Investigation into Automatic Music Transcription.* University of East Anglia (UEA), May. 2003.

[11] P. Desian and H. Honing. The quantization of musical time: a connectionist approach. *Computer Music Journal. 13(3):56-66*, 1989.

[12] Simon Dixon. *On the Computer Recognition of Solo Piano Music.* Austrian research Institute for Artificial Intelligence, Vienna, Austria.

[13] Dan Ellis. Lecture 10: Music analysis. *http://www.ee.columbia.edu/~dpwe/e6820/*, Spring 2005.

[14] Johan Forsberg. Automatic conversation of sound to the midi-format.

[15] S. Foster, W. Schloss, and A. Rockmore. Towards an intelligent editor of digital audio: signal processing methods. *Computer Music Journal. 6(1):42-51*, 1982.

[16] M. Goto. A robust predominant-F0 estimation method for real-time detection of melody and bass lines in CD recordings. *In Proceedings of the IEEE International Conference on Acoustic, Speech and Signal Processing (ICASSP), Istanbul, Turkey*, June 2000.

[17] Masataka Goto and Yoichi Muraoka. *Real-time beat tracking for drumless audio signals: Chord change detection for musical decisions*. Waseda University, Tokyo, Japan, 1998.

[18] Rémi Gribonval and Emmanuel Barcy. Harmonic decomposition of audio signals with matching pursuit. *IEEE transcactions on signal processing. vol 51*, Jan. 2003.

[19] Stephen W. Hainsworth. *Analysis of Musical Audio for Polyphonic Transcription*. University of Cambridge.

[20] Stephen W. Hainsworth, Malcolm D. Macleod, and Patrick J. Wolfe. *Analysis of Reassigned Spectrograms For Musical Transcription*. University of Cambridge.

[21] K. Kashino and H. Tanaka. A sound source separation system with the ability of automatic tone modeling. *International Computer Music Conference. 248-55*, 1993.

[22] Anssi Klapuri, Tuomas Virtanen, Antti Eronen, and Jarno Seppänen. Automatic transcription of musical recordings. *Proc. Consistent and Reliable Acoustic Cues Workshop, Aalborg, Denmark*, Sep. 2001.

[23] Anssi P. Klapuri. *Musical Meter Estimation and Music Transcription*. Tampere University of Technology, Tampere, Finland.

[24] F. Lerdhal and R. Jackendoff. *A generative theory of tonal music*. Cambridge: MIT Press, 1983.

[25] Matija Marolt. *Adaptive oscillator networks for partial tracking and piano music transcription*. University of Ljubljana, Ljubljana, Slovenia.

[26] Daniel McEnnis. Historical overview of transcription. *www.music.mcgill.ca/~mcennis/611P3Summary.pdf*.

[27] Giuliano Monti and Mark Sandler. Monophonic transcription with autocorrelation. *Proceedings of the COST G-6 Conference of Digital Audio Effects (DAFX-00), Verona, Italy, December 7-9*, 2000.

[28] J. Moorer. On the transcription of musical sound by computer. *Computer Music Journal. 1(4):32-8*, 1977.

[29] M. Piszczalski and B. Galler. Automatic transcription. *Computer Music Journal. 1(4):24-31*, 1977.

[30] M. Piszczalski, B. Galler, R. Bossemeyer, M. Hatamain, and F. Looft. Peformed music: analysis, sythesis, and display by computer. *Audio Engineering Society. 29(1): 38-46*, 1981.

[31] M. D. Plumbley and S. A. Abdallah. *Automatic music transcription and audio source separation.* King's College London, UK.

[32] Matti Ryynänen. Polyphonic music transcription using note event modeling, transcription examples.
http://www.cs.tut.fi/sgn/arg/matti/demos/polytrans.html.

[33] Matti P. Ryynänen and Anssi Klapuri. Polyphonic music transcription using note event modelling. *IEEE Workshop on Applications of Signal Processing to Audio and Acoustics*, 2005.

[34] Eric D. Scheirer. *Tempo and beat analysis of acoustic musical signals.* Acoustical Society of America, 1998.

[35] Vladimír Székely. *Képkorrekció, Hanganalízis, Térszámitás PC-n (hungarian).*
ComputerBooks, Budapest, Hungary, 1994.

[36] George Tzanetakis, Georg Essl, and Perry Cook. *Audio Analysis using the Discrete Wavelet Transform.* Computer Science Department, Princeton, USA.

1761212R0005

Printed in Great Britain
by Amazon.co.uk, Ltd.,
Marston Gate.